Stop writing books nobody reads

STOP WRITING BOOKS NOBODY READS

The dangerously effective way to write and publish a book that people read and refer

DEBBIE JENKINS

First published in 2022 by Intellectual Perspective Press

To find out more about our authors and books visit:
www.intellectualperspective.com

CONTENTS

PRAISE FOR STOP WRITING BOOKS NOBODY READS

Debbie's step-by-step process is so inspiring and so clear. Great focus on serving the reader. She's giving you a tested and proven approach. Every writer should take this to heart.

Derek Sivers, author of four short valuable books (so far)

I've worked with Debs before and she's the best in the business. Do yourself a favour and read this book before you type another word!

Callum Laing, CEO MBH Corporation PLC, 3x best selling author
(and still learning what I should be doing better)

If you want to write a short book that gets read and, more importantly, attracts more leads and clients for you and your business. A must-read.

Joe Gregory, Author, *Make Your Book Pay*

Fun, high energy, and packed with compelling insights, tips, and techniques – almost as good as working with Debs in person! I know because I've done it. Debs' advice will make your book easier to write, better, and more successful. If your book is already out, her tips can be applied to marketing your book as well.

Ann Latham, author of *The Power of Clarity*
and *The Disconnect Principle*

Debbie Jenkins uses her extensive experience in publishing to show you how to write a book that people read.

David Kadavy, author *Mind Management, Not Time Management*

Short, sharp and shrewd – a dazzling two-hour crash course in how to get your business book right first time.

Ian Shircore – pro ghostwriter, author of *Conspiracy, NLP and the New Manager* and many more

Witty, gritty, ruthlessly honest and incredibly helpful. It works.

Judy Barber, coach, facilitator
and author of *The Slow Coach Approach*

Start (and finish!) Debbie Jenkins latest book if you are thinking about writing a business book. She provides templates, practical techniques, and examples for how to create a book that works for your business.

Dan Kowalski, Solution Instigator at Plan A Thinking

If you're going to buy just one book on how to write YOUR book – this is the one! Debbie Jenkins pulls no punches.

Sue Haswell, Trainer, Coach, Psychotherapist, Author

Get your book out of your head and turned into a valuable asset for your business. Learn from the master!

Christine Ware, The Career Doctor

A whole new way for leaders to think about their business and create value for their clients.

Davina Ripton, Business Change Coach at Change Ready

Debs is the master that can guide you to writing a book people will read.

Tim Kist, FCMC, author and certified management consultant

Business author? Get into a bigger game... If you want to write a really useful book, and maximise its chances of getting read and referred to, Debs' short, friendly yet authoritative book is your inside track to professional-level performance. Its most important idea: a relentless insistence on adding value for the reader.

Andy Bass, PhD, author of *Start With What Works*
and *Committed Action*

A wake-up call. Get this book so that you too can avoid the so many pitfalls that authors too often fall into.

Dr. Maya Novak, mindful healing expert
and author of *Heal Beyond Expectations*

Frankly, you would be 'blonde,' not to pay attention to this industry-disrupting book! It will become a seminal and movement-creating book in time, that I know for sure!

Carrie Eddins, PR & Media expert, Connection Marketing Specialist
www.theblondepreneur.com

FREE FOR YOU

This book is enhanced with additional video content, checklists, playbooks, case studies and discussions. You can access all of this extra content by signing up at: www.ShortValuableBooks.com

This is book one in the "Ideas Into Assets" series. You'll also get advance reading of the next books in the series when you sign up plus more information, techniques, tactics, ideas about how to turn your thoughts into valuable things, along with free access to a community of creators and leaders.

We debated putting the word "that" into the title (Stop writing books *that* nobody reads) but in the pursuit of brevity, and with the assumption that you're reading this to learn, not check my grammar, we decided you didn't need that *that*.

BOOKS: STILL THE BEST WAY OF PROVING YOUR CREDIBILITY AND BECOMING A RECOGNIZED EXPERT

In one year, I wrote over one million words for other people. Most of those words should never have been written.

I've been in business book publishing for almost twenty years. During that time I've turned down thousands of books; I should have turned down even more.

I have coached, ghostwritten, rescued and recovered hundreds of books. Many of those books should have been much shorter.

The traditional publishing paradigm is wrong. It's too slow, too long and too expensive. The hybrid and self-publishing models mean anyone with some cash and know-how can get their ideas published. Many of those ideas are boring, repetitive and have no value to the reader. Everyone is writing a business book because they've been told to by writing, marketing and business coaches.

I'm a writing, marketing and business coach.

My advice? Stop writing books ... (that) nobody reads.

I vowed to never again write or publish a word that shouldn't be read.

I intend to fulfil that promise.

Why don't people read your book?

Because you wrote it with the same technique and mindset as we were writing books in the 1900s.

1900s book scene

Scarcity of information – usually traditionally published by one of the main 5 publishers

Selected special individuals – usually white men

Speed was not of the essence – we can wait

Size, weight and the tiniest font were indicators of value – opticians were doing a roaring trade

The only 'good book' was a magnum opus, a culmination of a lifetime's work – that few people read

It was an analogue world, with nuance, time to ramble, sidetracks and navel gazing – because people had time to read

You had time to write a legacy book – you had a job for life and a pension on the way

You had a waiting, with bated breath, audience – because they've bought some new candles to read by[1]

A committed publisher, who wined and dined their authors, putting the power of their marketing and PR team to work

---

2000s book scene

Abundance of information – you are not only competing with other books

Everyone can be a creator – even idiots and women[2]

We want it now – actually yesterday because we just screwed something up

Ideas weigh nothing, fonts are for trendsetting

By the time you've finished writing everything has changed, or at least 'blockchained'

It's a digital world, words alone aren't enough, in fact they are usually too much – 280[3] characters to get your point across because people are too busy to read more

Your book is a side project, something you're squeezing in between TikToking and taking the kids to school

Your 'readers' have probably not read a book since leaving school

You – yes, you – have to do it all, even with a 'traditional' publishing deal. Put your PR hat on and go shamelessly promote yourself.

If you are still thinking in the old paradigm – *write it, get it traditionally published and they will come* – you are screwed.

So, stop writing books nobody reads.

You don't need a long book published by a traditional publisher to get what you need. You need to get short valuable ideas out to your market in a professional way, as quickly as possible. That can be by blogging, writing articles, making videos *or* by writing a book.

And then you need to do it again.

Jason Fried, Founder and CEO at Basecamp: *"People don't have short attention spans, they have short interest spans."* If you don't interest people they move on, quickly. They won't read your long book. They won't understand your brilliant idea.

When you find a great TikTok[4] video you are encouraged to watch more by the same maker and more in the same field. TikTok does the searching and sharing for you. The average time spent on TikTok is fifty-two minutes[5] – to watch one-minute videos (of people doing stupid things). That means they watched fifty-two videos on average. Which really means some people watched a hell of a lot more! They are the super fans.

And don't think business people and leaders don't get drawn into the TikTok sixty second world. You've watched some, haven't you?

Your book is competing for attention from people with this mindset. People like you. You don't need to fight the trend, you could use it. Of course, there are times for a long legacy book, but right now people want atomic, shareable, valuable information – immediately.

Your book needs to be so interesting that they devour it, and then want the next one.

You want to be as moreish as the next Netflix series.

Bitesize, useful, life changing content.

Atomic, valuable, business-growing books.

Built around your expertise and their most important problem.

The book anti-patterns and their antidotes

When you're trying to reach your target audience effectively, nothing beats a well-written business book. But it's also tough to get right. Poorly written business books litter the virtual bookshelves. If you're serious about writing and publishing, and want to make sure that your message is heard above the noise, this book can help you accomplish your author brand-building goals and create an outstanding book that is virtually guaranteed to be picked up, and devoured.

But be careful, there are anti-patterns[6] about writing a book; these are the commonly shared and used ideas that produce a bad outcome. Here are a few:

- The proliferation of writing and publishing coaches, courses, workshops, retreats – mostly run by somebody who has written a couple of books and thinks they're an expert – is exacerbating the groupthink. They are delivering what looks like a good idea – **write a book in a week, mindmap and write in a weekend, self-publish** – but produces unreadable, unread books – at volume.

- The mistaken mantra that **your book is a calling card that will never get thrown away.** "Calling card" books get the same treatment as your calling card, put in a big pile and never looked at again! You don't want your book gathering dust on a desk holding down receipts, or propping up a monitor.

- The wishful thinking that just **"being" an author will get you the credibility you desire** is tricking smart people into parting with their money and time. If it was that simple just put your name on the cover of a book stuffed with blank pages[7] – it will be a lot cheaper and faster!

- The persuasive narrative that **everybody has a book in them** leading to wasted time, opportunities and cost. Yes, you might have a book in you, but do the people you want to reach read? Are they interested in a book as the delivery vehicle for your valuable information?

- The desire to overwhelm your prospect with more information, because *more* is better, and that you need the thud factor to make an impact! **People don't want information.** They want transformation, action, direction.

You want your book to be read because when people read your book:

- They will get the promise you made – they will get a transformation – their life will be better

- They will tell other people – write testimonials, buy copies for friends and colleagues, talk about your book on social media

- They will quote you in their books, in articles, online

- You will make an impact

To write a book that people read focus on the antidotes:

1. Make sure there's a business case before investing your time and money

2. Focus on what the reader needs to hear not what you want to say

3. Write value not volume

4. Think before you write

5. Use a framework for the process, not for the idea

6. Choose yourself, not the publisher

7. Produce a book that markets itself

I'm not going to say it will be easy, but let's at least make it worth your while ...

Everything in this book will work for all length books, and all styles. It's a process that has been proven to work. I encourage you to write short valuable books because you can quickly get atomic ideas out to your audience, get feedback and make an impact faster. If you want to write longer books this process will work, just know that you will need exponentially more time, resources and stamina.

Notes

1. The 1900s also includes 1999, it's not that long ago!
2. I'm allowed to say that because I'm a woman - and it's true. Though women and minorities are still under-represented in non-fiction: https://fortune.com/2020/12/20/women-bestselling-business-books-2020
3. The phenomenon of tweeting!
4. I am speaking as if I actually know anything about Tiktok. I don't. If you want TikTok advice speak to a young whippersnapper; if you want advice on how to use behavioural science and basic human psychology to get your stuff read, listen to us oldsters!
5. The average time spent on TikTok per day is fifty-two minutes worldwide: https://backlinko.com/tiktok-users, Brian Dean, Backlinko, TikTok User Statistics (2022)
6. Popular in software engineering, project management, and business management, anti-patterns help us learn from the stupidity of crowds.
7. Mike Winnet actually did this and got himself an Amazon bestseller.

1.

IT'S ABOUT BUSINESS, NOT VANITY – YOUR BOOK HAS A JOB TO DO

You might have already written a book, full of hopes and ambitions. Perhaps you've been published by a major publisher, and you're still not selling many books. I bet you've been doing all the 'social' stuff and it hasn't improved your business? The problem is your book needs a job to do, otherwise it sits around the house wasting space. You might not be able to revive an old book, but let's at least make sure your next book is read.

The question we're going to answer in this chapter is: what job should your book do and how do you make sure it gets read?

I am rabid about (a lot of things) your book being read – not *bought – for two reasons:*

1. You might decide to give your book away, do partnership deals, use the book to grow your business, or write a book for the person who will *buy your business*. Any one of these 'jobs' does not require the reader to *buy* your book. But they do need to read it.

2. I have *bought* a lot of books, but I haven't read them all. You could say I have a dose of the *tsundokus*, the Japanese term to describe a person who owns a lot of unread books. Fermat's Last Theorem[1] has sat spine-unbroken on my bookshelf for the last 20 years.

I deal with business books on a daily basis. I see the problems, meet the resistance and understand the people who want to write a book. If you're going to the pains to write it you want it to be read.

A book might not be the right vehicle to get you where you want to go. It might not get you the outcome you desire (you do have an outcome for the book, right?) It might not help the reader get what they need (you know what they want, really, really want?).

That being said, a book *could* be the right asset for your business. If you know who you are writing for, their desired need to move from where they are now to where they need to be, your business or personal outcome, and you can dedicate time to getting it done – then, yay! Write that book – and let this book help you.

In the first three chapters we'll be thinking about, and working to fill in your overall book Thought Leadership Canvas (TLC). The TLC will help you capture your thoughts about your book, the one reader and the way you can solve their most important problem. It will also help you organise your ideas into chunks for each chapter. The TLC is useful for all your business writing. Make yourself plenty of copies, one copy per book idea.

DOWNLOAD: You can get a printable copy of the Thought Leadership Canvas, or an electronic copy: www.ShortValuableBooks.com You will also find a short 'how to' video.

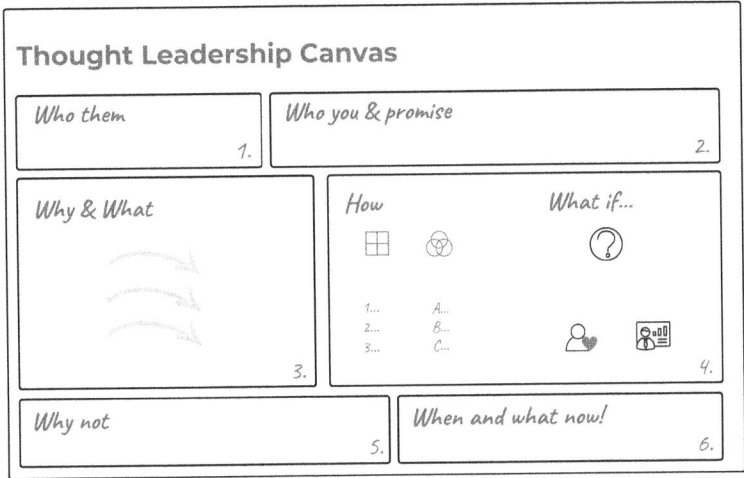

Thought Leadership Canvas

Who them	Who you & promise
1.	2.

Why & What	How What if...
3.	4.

Why not	When and what now!
5.	6.

There are six boxes on your TLC, you are probably familiar with the ideas behind all of them. We will use a TLC for the main book idea, and then a TLC for each chapter.

TLC Rules

1. Create as many canvases as you want – don't constrain yourself yet

2. You don't have to be correct – be creative

3. You are making assumptions – that's OK

4. You can have as many "thoughts" as you want – one thought per canvas

5. You can have one canvas for each book idea (or business model, idea, asset, article, app...)

6. You must have one canvas for each person – they are special

7. "Thoughts" are your way of making a transformation for one real person

8. Use post it notes to move ideas around

The Thought Leadership Canvas is just a model – there are other models.

I'll share a lot of models in this book, some are mine, others are from great thinkers. No model is perfect – hack it to work for you.

Everything we do in our business – marketing, social media, courses, events, offers, products, *books* – should have a job to do. I split that "job" into three parts: enhancing relationships, growing your business and dropping credibility clues. These jobs fit within The Asset Path® – the way experts grow their business, methodically.

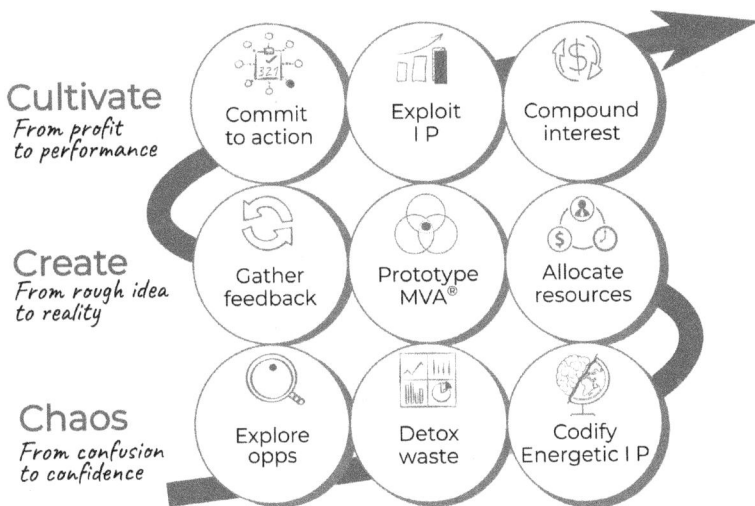

Cultivate
*From profit
to performance*

Commit
to action

Exploit
I P

Compound
interest

Create
*From rough idea
to reality*

Gather
feedback

Prototype
MVA®

Allocate
resources

Chaos
*From confusion
to confidence*

Explore
opps

Detox
waste

Codify
Energetic I P

In this book we'll be touching lightly on all nine of these circles in The Asset Path, in later books we'll go deeper.

How will your book cultivate relationships?

For your book to enhance the relationships with the people you want to influence your Most Wanted Response and theirs must be in synch. What's a Most Wanted Response (MWR)? **The MWR is the outcome from**

reading your book that makes both them and you happy.

The MWR lives in box 6 on the TLC. Download a full version to get more details. But you can't decide on the MWR until you know what stage of the relationship your book will be working at.

STAGES OF COMMUNICATION

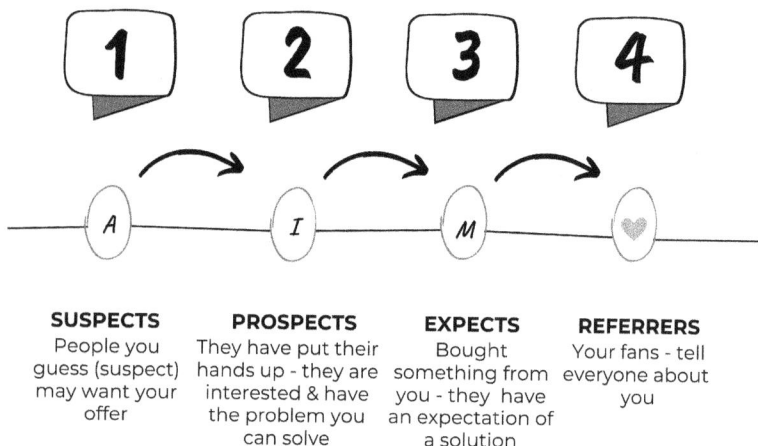

SUSPECTS	PROSPECTS	EXPECTS	REFERRERS
People you guess (suspect) may want your offer	They have put their hands up - they are interested & have the problem you can solve	Bought something from you - they have an expectation of a solution	Your fans - tell everyone about you

There are four stages of enhancing a relationship with a client or customer:

1. **Suspects:** The people you *suspect* may want what you have. You generate leads for your business by getting their **A**ttention (A on the image).

2. **Prospects:** The self-proclaimed prospects (they put

their hand up) are interested and want to get to know, like and trust you. You nurture your relationship with them by getting their Information, in return for giving them Information.

3. **Expects:** You deliver valuable services and products to people who come to expect a level of attention, and you reward their loyalty with more brilliant assets. You get paid for this – **M**oney – these are your clients.

4. **Referrers:** Make it easy, pleasant and profitable (not only in cash) to refer you, so they spread awareness and you don't have to shout about yourself. You've captured their hearts.

On the left you are paying for the relationship; on the right they are paying for the value you have provided. Your goal is to get people to the righthand side quickly and efficiently.

This is marketing 101. I call it AIM marketing (Attention, Information, Money), and without it you have aimless marketing. (This is my one and only apology for puns throughout the book!)

How will your book advance the STAGE of communication?

What job will your book do? Will it get attention and stop the scroll on the socials? Will you give it away in return for their email address to build your list of prospects? Will it be your first product to turn prospects into "expects" and receive money for value? Perhaps it will help current clients become evangelists and referrers? You decide. Your book can do any of those jobs (which is why books are so great).

Your book won't just enhance the relationships with the readers – it can also enhance your relationship with yourself. What will you learn? How will you grow? What will change within you? Who will you become by writing this book?

Once you've decided (for now), you can align your most wanted responses.

Example MWRs: know what the next step is, feel confident to take the next step, have a plan, install a process, have a system.

My MWR for this book is that you will know the steps to take to make sure your next book is read. That's probably your MWR too. Our MWRs are aligned. **Fill in your MWR in box 6 on your TLC. You will revise it later.**

Some people call this a "funnel", which I find quite disrespectful – I don't want to be funnelled, and I'm sure you don't either. When you think about enhancing relationships by capturing attention, sharing information, offering value (for money) and making your clients so happy they tell everyone else – that's respect!

How will your book grow your business?

Your book should produce an outcome for the reader (see the next chapter) and for you (grow your business).

What is an outcome? It's easy to get "activity" and "outcome" mixed up. We can be busy making, creating and doing things for our business – activity – and never reach the outcome we desire. Think about posting on social media, a busy activity that could produce an outcome, but frequently doesn't.

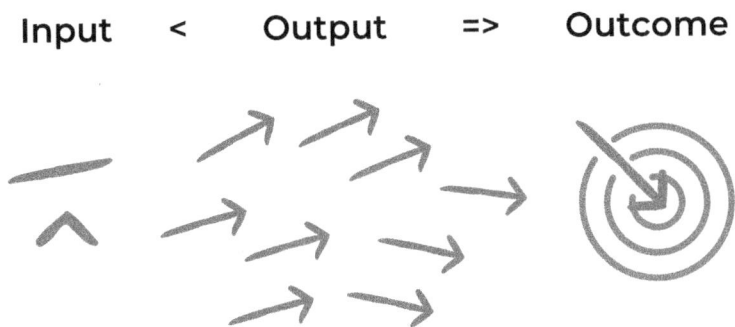

Input   <   Output   =>   Outcome

To be more successful in our business, and in writing books that people read, we need to reduce the inputs to only the necessary (no more cat videos, endless doom-scrolling, nor "one more course"ing), decide on the activities and actions we'll take (write a book, share the book, sell the book) so we reach an outcome (grow our business by making reader's lives better).

As Derek Sivers says in, *How To Live: 27 conflicting answers and one weird conclusion*[2]:

"You don't lack direction.
You have too many directions.
An open mind, like an open mouth, needs to eventually close on something."

What is the outcome of your book, for you? If you don't have an outcome for your book, how will you know if it was successful? How will you know if you need to course correct? I always consider these three outcomes when I am deciding what job my book has to do:

1. **Save you time/money:** Your book could be a useful onboarding tool so clients know what to expect when they work with you. You could use it to reduce ambiguity, so everyone understands your procedures or frameworks. Your book could be the best "credibility clue" reducing the time and effort needed to turn prospects into happy expects (clients).

2. **Generate revenue:** Your book could be a new product to sell; generate qualified leads to sell to; be part of an upsell or downsell for your other business assets and products; add extra value to existing customers; create credibility clues to increase referrals.

3. **Increase the value of your business:** If you are looking

to sell or find funding for your business, or you're looking for a partner then the value of your business is important. Your book can attract qualified leads, generate ongoing revenue and royalties, and can be an asset for many years – if you do it right.

> If you're still not sure try the Book Outcome Diagnostic where you can score your answers and decide what's most important to you right now:
> www.ShortValuableBooks.com

You'll see how closely connected your book's jobs are – they inform each other. You can't decide what part of the relationship you are enhancing without also deciding the outcome you want.

In the '90s I started a digital marketing consultancy in Birmingham, UK. I left a cushy, well-paid job and company car behind to see if I could make it on my own. I was ambitious, enthusiastic, and arrogant … It couldn't be that hard, could it?

We worked with consultants, coaches, trainers, speakers and expert advisors to grow their business while reducing marketing waste. Over the next three years we grew that company to twelve employees, clients from all over the UK, offices in the city, a chillax room for the team … I thought I knew what I was doing.

We'd "accidentally" done some things right because of the books we'd read, courses we'd attended and mentors who'd advised us. And because we believed in rapid iteration of ideas, we also had a few things that failed (we started the first virtual assistant company in the UK, about one year too early for the demand).

We named and trademarked our model and system – Lean Marketing™ – and I went around the country doing talks, speeches and keynotes. We systemised our own marketing (got to drink your own champagne, right?), wrote articles, were mentioned in the press, and were selected by large companies to fix their wasteful marketing activities.

Later we wrote the book about the methodology – *The Gorillas Want Bananas*[3] – and used it to give people a free or low-cost method of getting to know us. I sold it at the back of the room during events. It was for sale on Amazon when Amazon was still just a bookstore.

That book turned our business around, and became our number one credibility clue.

Decide what business outcome your book will produce.

How to help your potential clients make good decisions

When a potential client is considering working with you, or a potential reader is considering your book, they are looking for evidence that they can trust you, that you're a safe pair of hands, and that you have the experience and expertise to deliver what you promise. **I call these credibility clues.**

Credibility Clues are the signs and signals that you can solve the problem people have.

Prospective clients want to be confident in their decision to choose you. Your responsibility is to provide evidence, facts and proof to help them make a good decision.

You probably already have some credibility clues hanging around:

- Your framework, model or system that gets results for clients and solves their most important problem

- Testimonials on your website, in marketing materials and social media

- Past experience of being "selected" by industry bodies or authorities in your sphere – conference speaking, TED talks, keynotes, etc.

- Previous companies and clients you have worked with

- Case studies of the results you have helped clients (people like them) achieve

- Publications and media appearances

- Awards, accolades and certificates (not your "Little Dolphin 5m Swimmer" certificate!)

And, of course, a published book!

How do you use your book as a credibility clue?

You can drop credibility clues during three stages – pre-book, within the book and after publication.

Credibility clues during the writing and research stages:

- Signal on social media that you are writing the book. Mention it in your newsletter, when you speak to current and potential clients. Be real, show what's happening – the good and the bad. The clue here is that you are human.

- Share excerpts to demonstrate your expertise and show progress.

- Ask for feedback – "What do you think?" "What's more important to you?" "How have you handled this issue?"

- Gather and build an insiders group with whom you share extra information, they will feel connected to you, and could become beta readers. We will look at cultivating this group in a later chapter, **your Book Lovers Team**. Not only will this allow you to drop some credibility clues, but it should also make your book better and make the marketing easier!

Credibility clues within the book. More subtle (but not too subtle) credibility clues can be included within each chapter, try:

- "When I helped a Fortune 50 company … (achieve a brilliant result and save gazillions of dollars)"

- "I worked with Jim, CEO of (well-known company) …"

- "After speaking at the (well-known to your target audience) Conference …"

- "I am often called in to fix (problem your reader might have, and service/solution you want to sell) …"

- "I've gone through this same issue myself …"

Your author bio section is the most obvious place to name drop and mention companies you've worked with, and usually where most authors *only* drop credibility clues in a flurry of, "I'm great, buy me" enthusiasm. I can promise you that unless you drop credibility clues throughout they are very unlikely to even read the book, let alone your author page!

Case studies and case stories are of course brilliant credibility clues. Make sure they show a real transformation – how you moved the person from A to B, the same movement you are talking about in your book! Include facts, figures and feelings in the cases.

My favourite credibility clues are about you, the author.

Show your own journey from A to B – even the bad bits. I call these your FFFF credibility clues: Firsts, Failures, F*ck ups, Fight backs. We'll cover these in more detail in chapter five.

Make a note of your credibility clues on your TLC. They will go in box 4: your own story, case stories of client success, previous books you've written, your models, processes, frameworks and how they've helped clients.

Don't make the credibility clues too obtuse – it's not an intelligence test,[4] and you're not creating a credibility clue treasure hunt. Be bleeding obvious if you need to be. We're not talking about the Facebook "humblebrag" here. There's nothing humble about it – you are proud of what you've achieved and helped others achieve. And you're not bragging, you are providing credibility clues for potential new clients. You are building a bridge of trust to help them make a good decision. Your credibility clues help them make the decision for themselves!

Get your download of the Seven Book Job Recipes (includes free plus shipping, free ebook, low cost, low-cost with upsell, gateway, partner and sponsor).
www.ShortValuableBooks.com

Once you know what *you* want to achieve, the next question to consider is who are you writing for?

Notes

1. Fermat's Last Theorem, Simon Singh, Harpercollins Pub Ltd, 2002
2. Derek Sivers, How To Live: 27 conflicting answers and one weird conclusion, https://sive.rs/
3. The Gorillas Want Bananas: The Lean Marketing Handbook for Small Expert Businesses, Joe Gregory (my bro!) and Debbie Jenkins, Bookshaker, 2003
4. Seriously, drop clear and obvious credibility clues. You're not trying to create the "world's hardest cryptic crossword" (http://www.marcbreman.london/benchmarc/ Is This The World's Hardest Cryptic Crossword Puzzle? Marc Breman) – you're helping the reader decide to trust you.

2.

IT'S ABOUT THEM NOT YOU – WHAT YOU HAVE TO DO TO GET YOUR BOOK BOUGHT AND READ

The reader doesn't care who published your book, nor do they really care who wrote it (assuming you are a credible and reliable narrator). They only care about the ideas and what your book can do for them. They have so many things competing for their attention that if you fail to write your book for them (not you) they won't read it.

So, what do you have to do to get your book bought and read?

Do you remember that feeling when you look at an old group school photo, you scan the smirking faces, skip the teacher, check out the next row, until, 'Ah, there I am.'

When you see a group photo the first person you look for is yourself. You might be a bit embarrassed. (Who cut my hair? Mom. Why are my clothes too big for me? Hand-me-downs. Why am I sitting on my hands? Ink.) But there's a sense of satisfaction to find yourself in the photo. Why do we do this? Because it makes us comfortable – we are the centres of our own universe – we are special.

Who are you creating value for (this is marketing)?

I come from a very poor family of four kids. I was the oldest. I was the poorest kid in my class. I was also the shortest kid in the class, but that's not a surprise to people who've met me. If you had written a book back then for parents of thirteen-year-old kids, at secondary school, who were bright (I was a right swot actually!), lived in a city, had siblings and wanted to save to go to university, you might think my parents would be interested in that book. You'd be wrong. I was the poorest kid in the class. I could barely afford to go to school. My parents had no interest nor thoughts of sending me to university. They wanted me to get a job, so I could help pay for the food for my siblings. Your "avatar" book writing (and marketing) would have missed the mark. I am not an avatar. You are not an avatar, a persona, a figment of an over-active marketer's mind.

I am one very special person.

But I'm not alone. There were three classes in my year, and there would have been "the poorest kid" in every class. There were five "years" at my school, and there would have been a poor kid in every class in every year. There were twenty-odd schools in my region, and there would have been a poorest kid in every class in every year in every region. You get the point.

Forget avatars, personas, demographics. Forget about writing for groups of people. Write for one special person with one problem that your book can solve.

When you do this, everything else from today will get easier.

The secret to writing a book that gets read is to write for one reader.

You don't need to worry that, if you're only writing for Debs, you will miss out on all the other people because there are lots of Debs. I'm not alone in being a short-arse and coming from a poor family. If you wrote for the whole group (the avatar), I would never say: "Oh, that's for me." If you wrote for the poorest kid in class (one real person) who had to look after their younger siblings (most important problem), then I'd say: "Ah, there I am, that's for me." I would recognise myself. I would have searched and found myself.

I would also recognise other people like me and refer. I would share your book, because I would feel seen and would be able to "see" others.

How do you do that though? When you're writing, creating or you're marketing to one person it feels a bit scary. What about all the other people you can help? All the other thirteen-year-olds? (Think of the children!)

I know that scary feeling. I used to write for a "target group". It's a bad idea – let me explain.

Not knowing who *they* are and what their most important problem is will ruin your chances of success every time. You might have guessed who your readers should be, perhaps you did yourself a bit of psychographics and demographics, made up an avatar or persona, put yourself in their shoes – all the usual BS ...[1]

...and still people aren't buying what you're selling.

You can really only get close to having a bit of an inkling of what your readers/buyers/clients need when you get up close and personal, ask them (multiple times) and watch them in their natural habitat (sorry, getting a bit David Attenborough on you now).

Don't believe me? Listen to the science. We're pants[2] at guessing what other people want, think and need. (We're pretty useless at knowing what *we* want, think and need!)

In Nicholas Epley's book, *Mindwise: How We Understand What Others Think, Believe, Feel, and Want*, the University of Chicago Booth School of Business professor says we can understand what strangers think, believe, and feel only twenty per cent of the time, and with people we know we're not much better: "*With close friends you hit 30 percent, and married couples peak at 35 percent. Whatever you think is going on in your spouse's head, two-thirds of the time, you're wrong.*"

Now, think about your "prospects' head" how good are you at detecting their thoughts?

These imaginary people, with their imaginary thoughts and imaginary money?

Probably pretty crap, right?

And this is why you don't start with imaginary people, you start with one real person, you talk to them, ask them questions, listen to their feedback, get to really understand them – then you write for them, create for them, serve them – and you'll still probably be wrong – but maybe a lot less wrong.

Write for the ONE reader: not imaginary readers, with imaginary problems, imaginary 2.4 kids, imaginary wallets and imaginary money.

Who them

1.

Take a look at your Thought Leadership Canvas for your book. Up there, right at the start, the number 1 box, is your reader. **Fill in the name of one real person (who you would love to work with and should read your book),** and next we'll think about the pain they have, the gain they're searching for, and the transformations they'll get from your book.

What do they really want and why?

Real people have pains, problems and personal needs.

Real people work for their own and other people's businesses, and have troubles, disasters and hassles.

Real people have unspoken feelings, doubts and worries.

Your book must speak to one of these real problems, and show them how it can be fixed.

What type of problem or pain do they need resolving?
Most problems fall under the categories of health, wealth, relationships or self. They want to get fit, lose the weight, get a beach body. Grow a business, invest their money, save for retirement. Make friends, lead a team, bring up healthy kids. Get qualified, ditch the imposter syndrome, be calmer. Some people want to resolve all of those problems (or is that just me?).

The problem with problems is that some problems are more important than others. Solving the most important problem can have a domino effect on all their other problems.

What's their most important problem? Dr Richard Hamming[3] wrote; *"If you are to do important work then you must work on the right problem at the right time and in the right way."* An incredible intellect, he was known for gruntling his colleagues by questioning them on what they were working on, and whether it was an important problem. His follow up disgruntling question: *"if what they were working on was not important, and was not likely to lead to important things, then why were they working on them?"*

Time to be gruntled: **what is the most important problem for your one person? That's what you need to work on first.** Of course, when you solve that problem for them, they'll have another – which is why we write more books.

Most people have one of two types of problems: bleeding neck[4] or weeping wound. The bleeding neck problems are easier to spot and discuss – there's usually a lot of blood, and a certain "motivation" to find the solution. Bleeding neck problems: lose weight before I have another heart attack; get more clients now before we go out of business; stop sabotaging relationships before I get divorced again; understand my reason for being here before I die. They are urgent, they have a constraint (before), life will be pants if you don't fix them.

The weeping wound problems are a little trickier to spot, and frequently turn into bleeding necks if they're not resolved. Imagine limping along with a rock in your shoe, you can carry on up the mountain, but at some point you need to stop and fix the problem. Weeping wound problems: how do I get and stay fit in my fifties; how do I outsource so I can spend more time with my loved ones; how will I know I've lived a good life? They are important problems, which will get worse over time.

And you should also **look for the "invisible" problems** – what they're not telling you. The "4 a.m. Dave Brain" problems.[5] These are the types of problems that wake you up at 4 a.m. and switch on the "Dave" Channel in your brain. You watch reruns of all your favourite worry, disaster and confusion "shows". And then you do the same the night after. Invisible problems: am I good enough? Will I succeed? How do I know I'm on the right path? What if I make a mistake? How did they train the cat to sit in the bath?

How do you find out what their problems are? People search on Amazon, Google, Reddit, AnswerThePublic, Quora, in groups, etc. to fix problems or pains. If people aren't searching for these things then they probably won't find your book. They also read books, watch videos, listen to podcasts. If the category on Amazon exists, there are bestsellers with lots of reviews, and, if you have a better, simpler, faster, more elegant solution to the problem, then you might be on to a book that gets read.

Their most important problem is the most important question you should be answering. Anything else is your ego getting in the way.

Marketing matters: Use KDPSpy if you want to get some deeper understanding of what books are doing well on Amazon. There's a module on it in the full course.

The most useful way of finding out is to ask your ONE reader what they want, what's their most important problem. And how you can solve it for them.

Write down your one reader's pain and gain in box 1 on your TLC.

While you're talking to them, capture their words (video them if possible) as you discuss their most important problem (the one you're able to help them with, not their backhand, unless you're a tennis coach). Ask them open questions (how, when, who, where), future-pace them to think beyond the current solutions, check what they've already tried themselves. Watch and listen.

Use your TLC to capture your one reader's actual words and scribble their 'FROM A (Do, Be, Have)' in box 3 on your TLC.

Why & What

A   B
A   B
A   B
     3.

Write down as many as possible. Be precise. What are they seeing, noticing, sharing? How does the problem affect them? How does it affect their family, colleagues, employees?

For some examples of completed TLCs for books,

have a look at: www.ShortValuableBooks.com

A to Be transformations

Now, it's your job to work out the Bs (or BEs, who they become, it's not just about the "doing") for the transformations. This is what your book will help them achieve.

You can only do this well if you truly understand their problem, and are able to solve it. If not, stop writing your book.

Some 'Be' tips:

- Be descriptive (make it real)

- Use all the senses (see, hear, touch, smell, taste)

- Be relatable (feel, felt, found)

- Use their words (and connect to your lexicon, which we'll look at in chapter 3)

- Might, maybe, perhaps, if... to build rapport

- Not magical (believable)

- Create a lot of transformations – then select three

When you're writing the transformations that your book will bring, remember that people buy outcomes, results, solutions and gains, not the vehicle (coaching, consulting, guruing, your book).

> Watch a 15-minute video where I show you how to use a Thought Leadership Canvas here
> www.ShortValuableBooks.com

When you have filled in your A to B transformations for the overall book idea – for the most important problem your one reader has – it's time to think of an angle for the book, a value proposition, or in booky words: a title and subtitle.

The Tube Test for testing book ideas

Now you know what pain your one reader has, what solution they're looking for, and how your book can help them, it's time to wrap it up in a lovely title and subtitle for your book. Just like that! Easy-peasy! Right? Maybe.

It's perhaps the most exciting part of this whole creative process, and also the most difficult – naming your book.

Write down titles, subtitles and series titles every time you think of them. Make lots. Write down everything that comes to mind. You're going to wake up at 4 a.m. with a title idea. A friend will suggest something brilliant. You'll be inspired by a colleague, your mom or your cat. Make a huge list of titles, subtitles and series title ideas.

Run all your title and subtitle ideas through the "tube test". Who wants to sit next to somebody reading *Bomb Making for Beginners*? Or, *How To Tame Your Flatulence in Four Months*? Or, *The Psychopath Test*[6]?

The Tube Test: If your reader was sitting on the Tube reading your book would they feel proud? Or would they feel embarrassed? Because if they don't want to sit on the train reading your book, then there's no way you're getting a referral.

It's not only science. There is an art to it. All the following rules can be broken.

Naming rules to be broken

1. Rule number one: there are no rules. There really are no rules in titles and subtitles.

2. Be clear rather than clever.

3. Be aspirational rather than gloomy. You should be moving them away from the pain that they have (from your TLC), and give them a big dose of hope.

4. Your title and subtitle should show movement. You might be here, and this is where you can be if you've

read my book. They will be moved from their bleeding neck or weeping wound problems towards their glorious future.

5. Show benefits rather than features. The benefit of reading this book is you will know how to write your own book. So what? So that you can grow your business, make more money and retire to a farm in Spain. Obviously, that would be a bit of a long subtitle, but you see the difference between a benefit and a feature.

6. Be the difference that makes a difference, especially in crowded markets. If you are writing for a crowded market either make a promise that is outrageous that you can deliver, or take them off in a completely different direction to their expectations.

7. Be memorable and distinct. Be so memorable that your book will be referred, and be so distinct that when they look for your book they find it. After crafting a few titles/subtitles search for them in Amazon to see other similar titles available. If you get confused by the sheer volume of similar titles go back and try again. To prevent the same confusion happening to your reader you need a distinct title.

8. Use all the real estate that you have. Title, subtitle and series title all build to help your reader know this book is for them.

It doesn't matter what we think about the title or subtitle – the only thing that matters is what the reader thinks.

Marketing matters: If you wrote an article headlined with your title, would it attract the reader, and would they know what the hell you're talking about? Try it.

Share your title and subtitle ideas with your one reader. What do they think? Would they buy it? Does it offer hope of a solution to their most important problem? Would they sit on the Tube reading it?

I started sharing the title of this book (*Stop writing books nobody reads*) as my headline on LinkedIn well before I'd finished writing it. In the first two months I got 43 unsolicited remarks along the lines of: "Stop Writing Books Nobody Reads must be one of the best titles EVER! LOVE it." "Love the profile title Debs – already stopped me from writing a book!" Three of those people turned into clients. My book was already doing its job before it was written.

It's frequently at the end of the process where most books, articles, etc. are given a name. You might not find the right title and subtitle till the end – driving your editor, publicist and marketing people bonkers!

> **Marketing matters:** Don't keep your book writing idea a secret. If you have a newsletter list, tell them. If you don't, start one. Share your thoughts and ideas on social media. Message authors you admire, writers you want to quote and tell them about your book.

We know what's in it for us (chapter 1) and we know what's in it for them – how do we make sure they actually read it?

Notes

1. Behavioural Science, not the other BS.
2. For non-UK readers "pants" means rubbish, useless, dreadful. It's one of my favourite words.
3. R.W. Hamming, You and your research – a stroke of genius: striving for greatness in all you do, https://www.cs.utexas.edu/users/dahlin/bookshelf/hamming.html
4. I think it was Perry Marshall in the Sell or Die Podcast (www.sellordiepodcast.com) who first coined the phrase "bleeding neck"; I think I made up "weeping wound".
5. Sorry to all the Daves out there, but don't blame me, blame the BBC. "Dave" is a British television channel, which is available in the UK and Ireland.
6. That one is real: The Psychopath Test: A Journey Through the Madness Industry, Jon Ronson, Riverhead Books,U.S, 2012. A fun book to read, proving that any book naming rules are meant to broken.

3.

IT'S ABOUT VALUE NOT LENGTH – SHORT VALUABLE BOOKS ARE THE NEW PARADIGM

It can take years to write a good, "normal" book. Then it can take another couple of years for your publisher to get it out there. By the time it's published you've forgotten what you'd written, and it's probably out of date. Added to that, timely things need a fast response.

How do you get your ideas out there quickly and professionally?

The only way to get great ideas into the hands of waiting buyers and readers is to be fast to market. To do that we need to stop thinking about size, and start thinking about value.

I've noticed when I'm working with clients writing short books, at some point in the process the short books turn into a medium-sized book. Then that medium-sized book turns into a flabby large book. And if I'm writing big books with clients, a big book of 60,000 words accidentally turns into an 80,000-word book. You need to detox the waste, remove the flab, get your book fit for purpose. This is circle 2 in The Asset Path from chapter 1.

Your goal is to move the reader from A to B, to get that transformation for them, in as few words as possible, and only as many words as necessary. I suggest to (and constrain) my authors at Intellectual Perspective Press, that you should be able to write an atomic, valuable book in 20,000 words.

Value isn't the same as volume.

It's easy to add too many words; it's harder to only provide value.

Helping people get from A to B(e) with The DML Mental Model

Expert business owners and entrepreneurs have been told that they need a book to help them raise their profile, get more business, elevate themselves in crowded market places and position themselves as thought leaders. The tendency, and trap, is to emulate an author you admire, model their style and the way their book is built. While this isn't a completely bad idea (modelling success is of course a smart move) there are some problems.

There are plenty of ways to write a business book. You have to decide who you are writing for, the benefits they'll get from reading your book and how the book will help you and your business. If you get this wrong, or don't even consider the questions, you'll write a bad book that no one will read, waste your time, your money and miss out on opportunities. We've done all that work in the first two chapters. Go you!

We're going to look at a model for business book development: how to choose what type of business book to write and how to write a book that people will read.

You can download a copy of the Directions, Map, Landmark Communications Compass guide – with loads of examples: www.ShortValuableBooks.com

Helping people get from A to B

Imagine you want to get to the new restaurant in town, so you ask a friend to tell you how to get there. They send you a detailed list of turn-by-turn instructions to drive there from your home, a 20km journey. But you are at work, on your bike, two minutes away from the restaurant. How helpful are the directions? You really needed a landmark to help you – "head towards the train station and it's on the left".

Or perhaps you are new to the area and want some help finding your way around, getting to know the local environment, the best restaurants and where the good schools are. A manifesto on reopening the canal system won't be particularly helpful. Of course, later, when you have been there a few years you might be really interested, but right now?

Late at night you realise you've walked down a dark alley and are completely lost in the middle of a city, in what appears to be a not too salubrious area. A large scale, tourist map won't get you out of danger fast. You need a detailed, turn-by-turn, "get me to the closest metro station as fast as possible" solution.

There are different ways of providing information for different types of people, with different needs and at different starting points. There's a recurring word here: different. One system does not fit all.

To give good help you need to know where the person is now, where they want to go, why they want go there, how they plan to get there and whether you're going with them.

I first came across the idea of using Directions, Map or Landmark from my brother, Joe. He came across it in a book, *The Back of a Napkin*, by Dan Roam.

- **Directions-type books:** Directions books (how-to …) great for self-structured training, video courses, other books in a series i.e. "do this and then do the next thing in the list". If you have a team of people who take action, do the work and take the hassle off the client, this is the book you could write. How-to books are great for readers who are desperate for a solution, right now! They've probably got a bleeding neck.

- **Map-type books:** Map books (what and where to …) are great for people who have multiple products to sell and allow the customer to decide. Map books are for curious readers who will happily get stuck in and solve their own problems with a little help from you or your team.

- **Landmark-type books:** Landmark books (why to …) are for writers who want to lead, who are looking for followers and who are able to describe a bright shining opportunity, the top of a mountain that others want to climb. Your reader needs to be inspired by you and the issue. They are looking to follow an inspirational leader, and to solve their weeping wounds.

No one type is better than the other in absolute terms –they each have their role and place and time. I've found that expert author business books fall into about thirty per cent Directions, sixty per cent Map and ten per cent Landmark. So the vast majority of small expert business owners will end up accidentally writing a Map-type book. And that's where they get lost – in detailing the terrain! Not only that, but the flipping terrain changes on them. New legislation? Change the book. New methodology? Change the book. New markets? Change the book.

Your decision now will affect the way you outline, write and market your book. It will impact the title and subtitle. It will help you keep on track when writing, decide what not to include, and how to offer your services.

For example, this book is a Directions-type. I am showing you how to get your book written so that it will be read. I need to signpost it for you (tell you the next turn), keep your eye on where we're going (so you carry on taking the steps) and get you to your destination (a book that people read) without too many detours. This means I know what to leave out – I don't have to tell you how to turn your book into a course, or explain grammar and punctuation.

I advocate that you **write short, valuable Landmark or Directions-type books**, and leave the maps alone. Solve the weeping wounds and bleeding necks – leave the curious readers to someone else.

I have an imprint of Spain books that have kept me going financially when things got tough – well, when I had a marvellous mid-life crisis (how's that for a reframe?) and sold my boat, quad, houses, business, and got divorced. I wrote my first guide book (a map-type book) in 2005, because I couldn't find a book that covered the area where I had chosen to live. That 125,000 word book has gone through four editions over the last 17 years. Each time we had a mammoth job of updating, checking and fixing things because the 'map' changed. Each time I could resell the book to a captive audience, which was lucrative. But, I have vowed to not do a fifth edition, map-type books are hard work. The five Spain books brought me a recurring income when I wasn't working, and gave me the space to work things out.

If you're not sure what type of book to write, consider

the reader: do they need an obvious solution quickly? Directions-type. Are they interested in understanding the subject area? Map-type. Are they looking for inspiration for a bigger purpose? Landmark-type.

Try the quick quiz: *Should I write a Directions, Map or Landmark book?* at: www.ShortValuableBooks.com

Breaking the brain ⚡ world barrier

So you know you're going to write a Directions- or Landmark-type book (avoid Maps!), but how do you actually start? What's the mechanism for getting all of those ideas out of your head and into some sort of order? You create a **working outline**. This isn't your writing outline, we'll look at that in the next chapter.

A working outline is rough, messy, it's how you capture your thoughts, organise your ideas, identify your IP and map the value you're sharing.

Right now, we don't care about niceties, spelling, grammar – our only goal is to capture your thoughts, so we can organise them.

There are plenty of different ways and tools, such as:

- Google Slide Decks or PowerPoint

- Word Document or LibreOffice in outline mode

- Mind Map on Miro, Mural, etc.

- Trello Cards or Notion.so

- Post-it notes or physical cards

It does not matter what method you use (I am agnostic to the tool, and rabid about the process) just get it out of your head. You cannot get feedback on something stuck in your head.

I use a mixture of techniques for myself and with clients. I usually stay where they're comfortable. If you're happy with making slide decks, do that. If you prefer post-its, do that. There are no outline police.

I frequently use coloured physical cards. I've been writing speeches, books and workshops using the "card" method since 1998 – it's hard to break a habit. I write an idea on one side and details on the back, with notes for that chapter.

I've always got two, three or seven books on the go. I make a note on a card as I think of an idea. Then my cards turn into an outline on Google Docs. The good things about using physical cards: you can move ideas around easily; cards are limited in size so provide a physical constraint; I can quickly see if my deck is ready to be written; physical cards stop me from staying in my head. Bad thing: they only exist in one place and space – I need to go to my cards. Cards work for me – they don't work for everybody. Try cards if you haven't yet started or this is your first book.

Trello and Notion.so also let you pick up a group of items and move them around – but in this case, electronically. You have the freedom to easily change your outline structure on the go and you can access it from any device. I created a Notion template for my clients who are 'into' Notion, you can get a copy too.

Get your own copy of my Notion.so book outlining templates from www.ShortValuableBooks.com

---

Mindmapping by hand or digitally (I like Miro) helps you start with the big picture, and branch out to the chapter ideas. The Word outline method (or GoogleDocs, LibreOffice) tends to be for the writer-y types who are comfortable with a linear pattern of writing.

Currently, Google slide deck is my favourite method. I frequently deliver information to clients in webinars and my mastermind groups, and I can easily turn the slide decks into a book.

My workflow: create my slide deck outline, deliver it and make notes, get their feedback and then make adjustments into my slides. Did I confuse people? Move from ideas too quickly? I usually record my sessions, so I then get them transcribed and edited by my assistant. Those edited transcripts then become the chapters in my book.

I used the slide deck, deliver, edit method to write this book.

Find an outline method that gives you flexibility and freedom to move things around, make changes and get feedback.

Start thinking at a really high level – the big promise of the book. Then add the details.

You're working towards an outline so you can get feedback *before* writing.

After you've captured all your thoughts, it's time to organise them:

1. **Think of your reader's journey** – what does the reader absolutely need to know? What order do we give them the information so they get the transformation that they want?

2. **Then, on your book TLC,** add your overall model for the book. It will probably be your way of working with clients to help them get the result you promise – if you're a coach, consultant or trainer you will have your own way. It might be a model, a visual or a framework.

3. **Make a new Thought Leadership Canvas for each chapter**. Fill in the pain they have as they start reading this chapter, it will be different from the overall book pain. What are you solving in this chapter? What's the *chapter* A to B transformation?

4. **Fill in the actions, process or steps** they will take in each chapter on your chapter TLCs. What will they learn in the chapter?

5. **Think about a metaphor, hook or story for the chapter.** Will you be sharing your story or a case story (we'll look at how later)? How will you bring the idea in the chapter to life so they remember?

If you want to know how to develop your overall models or frameworks watch this short video, *Using*

the DML to Draw Your Business:
www.ShortValuableBooks.com

Line your TLCs up – can you see the journey?

Your chapter TLCs don't need to be perfect (don't get all anal-ytical on me), but they will help you when explaining and refining your book idea.

Your outline needs to move the reader from where they are now (that "bleeding neck" or "weeping wound" problem) to the promise that you're delivering (less blood).

IP per chapter, value per page and your lexicon

If you want people to read your book then there has to be a massive amount of value in it, they need to be blown away by the transformation you provide for them. How? By making it so different from anything else they've read that you create a category of one – you are the only person they think about when they have the problem you solve.

Your Intellectual Perspective: Each chapter needs to include your intellectual perspective, your IP. You are a thought leader, a consultant, a trainer, a well-read, experienced professional. Make sure you encapsulate that perspective in:

- Stories, case stories or metaphors

- Models, visuals or frameworks

- Actions, processes or steps

- And your lexicon (see later)

You've already been adding these to your chapter TLCs. Now go back and see if any chapter is missing some IP. Of course, you will (and should) reference other people's models and ideas (and start referencing them immediately. Don't leave it till the end). But you aren't a reporter, curating what other people have said and done. You are a leader. Develop your own IP.

I want you to have this in your mind all the time: every page, especially in a short book, has to add value. No filler pages. Keep asking: "What do they need to know? What's the value on this page?"

Your rough outline will show a massive value structure.

I want you to feel scared to give so much value away.

I want you to worry that if you give all this value in a book there will be no reason for them to work with you. They could just do it themselves ...

And then I want you to realise, every person who gets

their transformation from your book – who gets what you promised, and more – will tell at least one other person. This is how you build marketing into the heart of your book. If it worked for Facebook[1] then ... (it's probably immoral).

Value also means making them think, not doing the thinking for them. Be obvious. Nobody's got time to work things out for themselves. That's why you're writing your book. You don't have to do the thinking for the reader, but do make sure they're thinking about the right things!

Sue Haswell, Owner of Big Results PR & Marketing says: *"I gave away my whole process on how to write a press release in a book and sold loads of the books. It didn't lose me any work – in fact I gained more because people booked on my training courses after they had read the book. And did that lose me work? Nah – they still asked me to write the press releases afterwards too – but I got better information from the clients to be able to write the releases even quicker!"*

Marketing matters: Give extra value for free from a book landing page. You could give a free chapter, a quiz, a test, a diagnostic, checklist, cheat sheet or resource. These free assets for the book work in a combined effort to sell the book. More important, they get your book readers to identify themselves (email address and name) in order to get access.

You'll find at least twenty valuable resources when
you come to: www.ShortValuableBooks.com

Your lexicon: Your lexicon is your intellectual perspective. It's not just for writing – it's also for your business, for everything you talk about in the future, your marketing strategy, messages and landing pages. Your lexicon is the words and phrases that you want other people to share about you. Your lexicon, the words and phrases that you always use will become your intellectual perspective, your intellectual property. Other people will quote you.

There are also words and phrases that you will never use.

Your lexicon:

- Educates the reader about your intellectual perspective

- Frames the conversation and demonstrates value

- Creates a hook, something for readers to hold on to

- Claims your perspective

- Shows how you are different

If you don't name your ideas other people will, or they'll forget about you...

Some of my examples:

- Chaos is a feature, not a bug – I use it frequently when speaking to a client in those first few calls, when they're feeling a bit nervous.

- Minimum Valuable Assets® – This is a registered trademark. I am against minimum viable products[2] for thought leaders and consultants. Why? Because a viable book could just be a physical book with blank pages stuck in it; that's a viable product, but it doesn't have any value. So for consultants and thought leaders, a minimum viable product doesn't work. A Minimum Valuable Asset works a lot better.

- The Asset Path® – I lead people through a path of building business assets, not a one-off and done thing.

- Stop Starting, Start Stopping® – I've been saying this for twenty-five years, but I don't actually listen to myself.

- Actopedic – search on Google, I'm the only person in the world who uses this.

When you have a lexicon, special phrases, two or three words that you've put together, or a made-up word, you can register them as trademarks. And while the legality of registered trademarks doesn't completely protect you from the whole world, it does, however, help you stake a claim.

- **Make two lists: will use and won't use.** The words that you won't use are almost as important as the words that you will use. You'll start to notice reactions when you're speaking to people and getting feedback. When you say something that resonates with them, quickly make a note. When you say something that makes them react negatively add that to the opposite list.

- **Keep building the list as you write.** A really good lexicon will probably be about twenty phrases and words that you will use, and maybe a hundred that you won't. The ones that you will use are the most important ones.

- **At edit stage, do a search for the "bad" words and replace them.**

- **Search for your good words and make sure they are clear and frequently used.** The best lexicon words don't need a description. Stake that claim to them, because you want people to use your lexicon properly.

Using a phrase once is not a lexicon, that's an accident.

The brilliant thing about lexicons is once you have this list of words and phrases that you always use it will help you write the description, sales pitch, the landing pages, all your marketing, your messages, your emails and your signature file. You will have coherent branding that stays on message.

During early calls with my client, Gareth Helm, I noticed he frequently used nautical terms when discussing marketing. Gareth is an experienced marketing C-suite player, who has worked for companies such as McDonald's, Mars and Innocent Drinks. He loves his nautical terms: *"I was naturally using a lot of nautical words and you picked up on this which then became a theme, my metaphor."* Gareth developed his whole framework around them – the ANCHOR factors. He's built a diagnostic and written a book, showing the C-suite how to get the most from their marketing hires.

Marketing matters: Now you've got a working outline (captured thoughts) don't keep it to yourself – share it. You need to get feedback. Share your scrappy outline with friends or colleagues, your social media, closed groups and of course your one reader. Talk them through your outline, watch their faces, check for comprehension – are they interested in finding out more?

If you get a great response to your working outline and suggested titles and subtitles, then it's a goer to the next stage. If not – stop. Don't go racing ahead until you are eighty per cent sure you're on to a winning idea.

So you know why you're writing a book for you, who you're writing it for, and now you've broken that first barrier and sketched out a working outline with your IP and the value you'll be adding. So, you just get on and write, right? No, a bit more thinking *and testing* so you can sculpt a writing outline.

Notes

1. David Kirkpatrick, The Facebook Effect: The Inside Story of the Company That Is Connecting the World, Simon & Schuster, 2011
2. Defined in 2001 by Frank Robinson, and popularised by Eric Ries.

4.

IT'S ABOUT PREPARATION, NOT RACING AHEAD – SAVE YOURSELF TIME, INVEST IN YOUR THINKING

Many authors (especially first timers) race straight into writing. They haven't tested the working outline, don't have a plan for writing, haven't considered the front matter and end matter, they'll just throw it all in later. The problem is that later means unravelling a lot of work, rewriting, changing direction and probably wasting a lot of time.

How can you reduce writing time by doing a bit more thinking and testing?

You need to convert your working outline (captured thoughts) into a writing outline (organised ideas), and then write to that.

A writing outline is refined: your thoughts and IP are codified, organised, corralled, ready to be fleshed out. A brilliant writing outline shows the reader the journey of the book, is interesting and intriguing, and, most important, allows you to easily write your book.

The most important things are most important

Your writing outline will turn into a table of contents for the reader, and the table of contents is one of the most important elements that can help people decide whether to buy your book, or not.

When a reader decides to buy your book and to read your book, they put it through a series of "tests". Your book has to pass all the tests.

1. **Cover:** The first test is the cover. Does this look professional? Interesting? Has it grabbed my attention? Would I be happy to sit on the Tube with this cover visible? (Remember the Tube test.)

2. **Title and subtitle:** Is this book for me? Do I want what it's offering me? Is its promise going to solve my problem? Is it going to get me from A to B? Can I see myself? (The school photo test.)

3. **Description:** On Amazon, online bookstores or the description (back cover). The reader is thinking, do they understand me? I am so bloody special – is this book just for me? Does the writer understand my big pain, my weeping wounds, my bleeding neck?

4. **Table of Contents – TOC:** On Amazon potential readers can click "search inside" and see the table of contents. They're asking themselves, what do I learn?

Have I already learned something from the table of contents? What does that mean? What does chapter three mean? I really need to know more! The TOC should leave open loops that will be relieved by reading your book.

5. **Sample:** Then people read a sample (on Amazon, or flicking through in a bookshop). They'll ask themselves, is it readable? Do I like the style? Do I like the writer? Is this a book that's going to make me happy after I've read it?

The TOC comes from your writing outline, and is important, not only because it helps the reader decide to buy your book – it also helps you to write it.

Get the Six Chapter Outline Recipes (using the Directions, Map, Landmark outlines plus seven examples) www.ShortValuableBooks.com

Get your TLCs and working outline notes together and write the **writing outline** in your favourite writing tool (probably a word processor).

Now it's time to refine, fix and create.

Your writing outline needs to include the working titles and subtitles (if you haven't yet narrowed it down to "the one"), your SCQ statement for the book (coming up), a very simple one sentence introduction, a list of chapters each with an opening paragraph SCQ. Use bullet points for the main ideas in each chapter, your IP and value.

Opening paragraphs for the book, and each chapter: Write a transformational type paragraph at the beginning of each chapter in the outline. You may remove this later, but the readers need to know what you're promising in every chapter and how you're fixing their weeping wound or bleeding neck. Keep it short for now, we're still in the outline stage; you will elaborate on it when you're writing the book.

There's a brilliant methodology, **SCQA**, created by American author and consultant Barbara Minto,[1] that I recommend you use for each chapter, the introduction and for the conclusion. Minto recommends that all communication should be in the form of a "pyramid". Your Answer comes last. Build the pain first with the Situation, Complication and Question.

- **Situation** – where are we now? Meet the reader at the problem. The situation changes as they read through the chapters. Check on your TLC to make sure you understand their situation – in the A column in box 3.

- **Complication** – agitate the pain so they feel a desire to take action.

- **Question** – what should we do? Join the reader at the question.

- **Answer** – these are your main points in the chapter, what you need them to know and understand.

Example, for a chapter for a book:

- **Reader's Situation**: I need to grow my business.

- **Complication**: There are a lot of ways to grow my business. There are a lot of business experts guruing about. I might pick the wrong team and get confused. I might waste my money on the wrong programme or system.

- **Question** they might be thinking: "What asset should I make first to grow my business?"

- **Answer:** The answer to their question is found in your chapter.

Use SCQA for each chapter. This book is written in that style. Go and read the opening paragraph for each chapter. Can you see the formula? **You don't need to leave the SCQ in your final draft, use it as a lens to check that you have delivered on the promise for the chapter.**

For the introduction and conclusion we add a bit of "why you" and "why now". Why you adds authority and gives them a reason to read on. Why now gives them some urgency to read the book. You have to build that urgency up. The why now could be: new technologies to take advantage of and lots of competitors entering the market, so, if you don't stand out now, when will you stand out?

You can find templates for how to outline your book
at www.ShortValuableBooks.com

Take the reader on a journey

I've got some rules – because I've always got rules – for the
outline and structure of your book which will be visible in
the table of contents:

- **Tell the story of the book (the journey for the reader):**
  If you're writing a Directions-type of book then they
  need to know the steps. They should be able to see
  that journey. If you're writing a Map-type book (please
  don't), they need to see that the map is complete,
  that you haven't missed a bit. And if you're writing a
  Landmark-type book, they need to see that where you
  are taking them is aspirational, and possible.

- **Be intriguing and interesting:** No more "conclusions"
  – we're not writing science experiments at school. Give
  the reader something a bit more exciting than
  conclusions and introductions. You don't even have to
  say chapter one, chapter two, etc. You can call them
  whatever you want as long as it's useful.

- **Make it useful:** If the reader only read the table of
  contents, would they be happy? Would they have

learned something? If you can provide value in a table of contents, then the reader will be confident that you're going to provide value in the book. It'll convince them to buy your book. They will be confident there will be less blood!

- **There are no rules**: Be creative. Some books have long tables of contents, some really short. But remember the table of contents influences a potential book reader to decide to read your book. Give them a reason to read your book.

An outline isn't just the chapters – it's all the other stuff too.

You're writing a book that will be read by a population who are inundated with shiny things competing for their time. So, keep it short, about 20,000 words. Yes, you need front matter and end matter, your author bio, reviews, most wanted responses and we need added value.

Some rules to be broken:

1. **Front matter and end matter shouldn't be longer than your book matter:** Cut out the preface and foreword, the thirty book reviews, acknowledgements of your junior school teacher, and the rambling author bio and CV. It's all too much. The vast majority of your front matter goes at the end *unless* it's adding value to the reader.

2. **Use the space to provide credibility clues:** Use front

matter to provide credibility clues to demonstrate why you are the authority on this subject matter. A foreword has to be a credibility clue for you and for your book, not a thinly veiled "look at me" from the foreword writer. Add reviews for the book if it's a review that your target market will trust. The reviewer needs to be credible to your readers.

3. **Most Wanted Response up front and at the end:** Your MWR needs to be at the beginning of the book because that's the number one thing you want your reader to do that will lead them to *their* MWR. Go back and have a look at your book TLC for your MWR for the book. A Most Wanted Response could be "download extra valuable chapters to get your result faster". This MWR call to action needs to be within the first ten per cent so that it will be seen even if the reader doesn't buy your book.

   The challenge with selling books through retailers, like Amazon, is that the retailer has all the customer data and you get nothing. You have to ask the reader to give you their data. And in order for them to give the data you have to give them something in return: that is the "Most Wanted Response handshake".

4. **Ask for reviews:** We all want reviews. In the book ask for a review and tell them how to do it. Put this page near the end, because that's the best time to review a book. If you don't ask for it, people will forget because they are busy. I'll be asking for a review later!

5. **Where's the extra value?** Be generous. The book is just one tiny part in your bigger business garden. Where else can they go and get some more of your stuff? I suggest you be really generous. Not everybody will take you up on the extra value offer but be generous: extra free chapters, a free course, recycle some of your previous work, checklists, cheat sheets, videos. The benefit when you are generous and give stuff for free is that in order for them to get it, they're going to give you their email address – a Most Wanted Response handshake. I am offering you tons of extra stuff for free at www.ShortValuableBooks.com All I ask in return is your email address.

6. **Your author bio should be interesting and about them!** Put your author bio at the end. Why? Because people just don't care how much you know and who you are until they know that you care about them. You should be demonstrating that you know what you're doing and talking about throughout the book. Don't just splat your CV, or LinkedIn profile in.

   My author bio could be: "I'm Debbie Jenkins, BEng. I've got a degree in electronics and I've run a business for 25+ years…" That reads more like a boring CV. But if I were to write: "I've helped hundreds of people like you get their book written. And this is how we can do it together…" the bio is about them. If you want your reader to read your bio, make it interesting, make it about them.

Wherever possible, put your front matter at the end. Use the space to provide credibility clues, add value and ask for the Most Wanted Response.

Get feedback (before you even start writing) from your Book Lovers Team

Is it time to write yet? No.

You now have all the big chunks in place: the main chapters outlined, your SCQs for each chapter, bullets from your working outline added in, a scrappy drawing of your model, notes for case studies and your story. You'll probably have 2,000 to 3,000 words if you've done this step diligently. You'll be excited to start writing, because you can see a strong outline. But stop.

You are not a reliable judge of your own work.

Do not go from outline to writing unless you're ninety per cent happy with your outline. And that means getting some feedback. If you go ahead and write without testing your outline you might write stuff that you don't need, go too far off course and end up having to do big course corrections. Don't waste time or energy. Invest in getting feedback. Gathering feedback is circle 6 on The Asset Path, and you'll revisit this circle many times.

You'll already have started telling people about your book

idea, your title and subtitle and asked-for case studies. Now it's time to grow your Book Lovers Team. These people are bloody lovely.

Start building your Book Lovers Team (BLT) – you're looking for about 100 people who will help you now and at launch. You need a group of people to: read your outline, share your messages, write reviews and tell you when you're being stupid!

1. Decide "where" you will collect them. Set up a WhatsApp group, add them to your mailing list, make a group in Gmail. Make it easy for yourself by herding them.

2. Marketing is about adding value. What value can you provide for your BLTers? Can they get discounts, extras, free books? Be generous.

3. Grow the team over time. Encourage your fans, clients, past clients, colleagues, friends to join.

4. Communicate regularly with them. Keep them in the loop, give them the inside scoop.

5. Thank them – a lot.

I have some templates you can use for attracting and keeping your BLTers in the loop, get your own copy of

---

Book Lovers Team Dashboard,
www.ShortValuableBooks.com

At this stage – writing outline – all you need from your BLTers is to tell you their first impression on the title, subtitle and outline: would they want to read it? Do they have any suggestions for changes? Have you missed anything?

Fix their suggestions (if you agree) then you can start writing.

I have "rescued" hundreds of books over the last fifteen years. The single biggest problem I have found is that the author is writing in isolation, stuck in their ego chamber. Involve your BLTers.

We've converted our desire to write a book into an idea for a business asset, that a specific person will love to read. We've gone from a rough, working outline to a refined writing outline, and we've got some feedback to test our hypothesis. Is it time to write yet?

Notes

1. Barbara Minto: http://www.barbaraminto.com/ and her book, *The Pyramid Principle: Logic in Writing and Thinking*, Prentice Hall, 2010

5.

IT'S ABOUT YOUR DEDICATION TO PROCESS, NOT YOUR LITERARY PROWESS – NO BLANK PAGES, NO WRITER'S BLOCK

You might already write blog posts or articles, perhaps you've even written ebooks and a book in the past. You're good with words ... The biggest fear for writers (after not being read!) is not being written. It can be difficult to get started, maintain a writing rhythm, work out how (and if) to reuse old material, and actually finish what you started.

What if there was a way to guarantee you'd never have writer's block, and get your book finished?

People get stressed looking at a blank page. They don't know where to start. The benefit of a tested, detailed outline is that you're never going to have writer's block.

Once you have a really good outline, you write confidently

to the outline knowing that you're writing towards the right outcome.

You can change the outline a little, you might spot new things or you might want to add new stuff. The outline is basically a prompt for the page in order to get you to start writing. This way you know what you need to write next.

Speak, write, uncover hidden assets

My writing rules (don't break them!):

1. **Write quickly, to each point in your outline:** Don't agonise, get it down, get the clever ideas out of your head.

2. **Write intro and conclusions last (and don't call them that):** If you write them first, you will almost certainly have to rewrite them. When you write to an outline you know roughly the direction your book is heading; however, you will do some course corrections as you're writing. If you write the introduction first and state that you're going to make these three points, but along the way the third point changes, you will have to go back and edit the introduction. So introductions and conclusions are always written last. You can outline and put some notes in for your introductions and conclusions, but wait until the end to fully write them.

3. **Don't edit until you've finished writing:** This is the hardest rule for me, it's the hardest one for my clients, but do not edit until you finish writing. Edit-mode and write-mode are two different activities. When you're in writing mode, you are in a creative, expansive, thinking mode. When you're in editing mode, you're in a cut it back, fix it, make it better mode. These are two different modes. And if you try and do them at the same time, it'll take you twice as long to finish.

From a logical point of view, if you write *and* edit as you go along the first few chapters will get progressively better, but the later chapters get fewer and fewer edits. That's not what you want. You want every chapter to be edited brilliantly. So write first and edit after.

4. **Don't stop for research – use the XXX method:** When you're in the "writey" flow, don't allow thoughts such as "What was that study about time management again?" "What was that research on keto diets?" to stop you writing. Do not stop to research. Just put triple X together ("XXX") and carry on writing. You'll never find three Xs in a word so, when you've finished writing, search for all the triple Xs and go fix them. When you're in writing mode do not open the web browser to do a bit of research, do not go down any rabbit holes because you will lose a lot of time.

5. **Value per page:** This means every page – especially with shorter books – has to be valuable. We need to

get rid of the clutter, remove the long explanations, reduce the rambling. My ambition for you is that, when a person opens your book, whatever page they open it on, they will find value.

6. **What's your IP – special you – minimum one per chapter**: Your intellectual property, or intellectual perspective (your way of thinking about the world that's going to help the person reading get what they need to make a transformation) needs to be evident in every chapter. If you don't have an IP in the chapter, ask yourself, what's the chapter doing? If the chapter is just mapping information and you don't have a special perspective on it, then you either have to find a special perspective, or you have to get rid of the chapter. If you don't have your IP in a chapter, you're just regurgitating other people's stuff. Don't do it!

Which brings me to the three ways that you can write a book. Choose which one is right for you.

1. **Talky Peeps:** You're a talkative person like me? Record yourself on the phone, disputer [sic], or dictaphone (depends how old you are), and then send it off to transcription. I use this methodology: record, transcribe and edit. I suggest you use artificial intelligence transcription, because it's cheaper and faster. I use Otter.ai. Then you edit it because AI transcription is frequently funny.[1] You can also dictate directly into a word processor.

2. **Writey Peeps:** Writey people write. If you're a writey type person, you like the tippety tap of the keyboard, so go ahead and start typing. Write it. Get it out of your head.

3. **Upcycley Peeps:** Maybe you have workshops or courses that you want to reuse and recycle, past articles and blogs, unfinished books to take chunks from. Upcycley people can recompile assets and figure out where they fit in their outline. Your edit job will be to join up the dots, find out what's missing and then fill in the gaps.

Don't upcycle any old pants! Remember your book has a job to do. Respect the reader. Provide real value. Don't be a lazy armhole (as my mom would say).

When you have an outline you are not starting with a blank page. You have something to give you prompts to get you moving forward.

Actually writing, getting the words on paper

Not finished writing? Not started writing? I know, it can be hard to get going, keep going and finish. Here are some ways of getting accountability, motivation or traction.

For all the things that you want to turn into a habit rather than a "just did it because someone was shouting at me", try the three handstands habit:[2]

1. What's the minimum you can do? One hour writing? Fifteen minutes?

2. What's the frequency you will do it? Every day?

3. How will you ensure you get it done? Accountability group? Habit stacking?

4. How will you know you're doing well? Where's the feedback mechanism?

You don't have to do it all today. But you do have to keep going. It's really important that you get the writing done because you can't go on to the next stages.

In one of my groups, Short Valuable Books, a couple of the members took it upon themselves to set up an accountability group. They would meet up on Zoom, in two minutes make a commitment to what they would achieve in the next hour, then get writing. They called it the Pyjama Club because it started at an ungodly hour. I joined them – it was amazingly useful for writing this book.

Tolerations and XXX method

Keep a running list of things that are annoying you about your book. You can keep a running list of things that annoy you about your life too, but that might be a very long list.

Batch your "fixing" things time because you don't want to fix as you write. Fixing things is different from writing things. You need to batch those jobs because then you can stay in one mode longer. It's the context switching from writing to editing from fixing to writing where you waste most of your time and you lose all these lovely brain cycles.

- **What needs to be fixed/finished/fecked off:** As you're writing you will spot things that you're going to have to tolerate for a while until you get to the editing stage. These will be things that you haven't quite finished, that need to be fixed, or they're not quite right.

- **Edits:** If you get to a sticky spot during writing just put an XXX. If you're unhappy with a section, put an XXX. There might be sections that really need to be edited better, you wrote them in flow, you weren't feeling comfortable with them, or you reused writing from other places, so they need rewriting and editing to fit the new style.

- **Research:** Add any research that you need to do to your tolerations list. Maybe you mention statistics that you need to research and credit a source.

- **Word choices:** Add word choices that need to be

checked in your lexicon. I like the rhythm of writing in threes. However, I can't always write in threes. Sometimes I can think of two things but I can't think of a third thing. So I put XXX or a boring word, and come back to it later.

- **Search and replace:** If you've used a client's name all the way through as a case story and later you want to change it to protect their innocence or guilt, add that to your tolerations list.

Put your writing hat on and write. Don't accidentally become an editor.

Writing about yourself – FFFF

You can get heavily criticised if you are too promotional when you start writing about yourself. The same goes for writing about your programs, the things you're doing or your books. Obviously, you want to tell people about what you're doing in your books and why you are who you are. But if it appears too promotional people get agitated. Here's a technique for writing about yourself inside the book. Use the four F system.

1. **Firsts:** Write about the first time you did something, understood something or felt something. Write about the first time you found yourself in the same position your reader may be in. When did you first understand the problem you're writing about, and come up with a solution?

2. **Failures:** Write about your failures. What did you try that didn't work? What else did you try? You want them to remember that you're just one or two chapters ahead in the book. You're the guide, not the guru.

3. **F*ck Ups:** What did you do that was completely stupid in hindsight? How big a screw up was it? Be honest and revel in the gory details! This way, people will start seeing you as a real person.

4. **Fightbacks:** How did you fight back from failures and f*ck ups? Who guided you? What elixir did you find and you are now offering to the reader? How did you come back from any brink of disaster? Write this so that readers won't think that you're just a failure; you've only done things for the first time and you've screwed up a lot. You actually want them to see how you fought back from adversity. You're demonstrating that while you might have had a failure, or you might have done something really wrong or stupid that you can fight back, and they can too.

Rather than people thinking that you're promoting yourself, they will be relating to you, because the easiest way for people to relate to others is if they realise they're not perfect human beings either. You can use the FFFF credibility clues in the introduction chapter to build rapport and demonstrate that you're not superhuman, you have flaws and you've been where they are now. It gets you off the pedestal and into the arena.

You may use your own story as arcs in the book, as open and closed loops, or as a thread that goes through the whole book. If you put some of these FFFFs in, you will get rapport with the reader. They won't feel that you're promoting *to* them.

Story is really important for humans. We are storytelling animals[3] and we just love a good metaphor or story. It's how we learn. Jonathan Gottschall draws on the latest research in neuroscience, psychology, and evolutionary biology, *"Did you know that the more absorbed you are in a story, the more it changes your behavior?"* So tell your story, engage the social side of the reader's brains, bring them into your real world, and they might change their behaviour and do what's good for them.

Writing about others

One useful mechanism in books is to tell case stories. "Case studies" is too clinical. We're not studying them; we are telling their story so we can learn from them.

When you're interviewing somebody for your book use the case story formula:

- What was happening to them before they did the thing you're suggesting?

- What specifically did they do?

- What's happening for them afterwards?

Case stories show the journey – the same journey you're explaining in the book, and in each chapter – the A to B transformation.

Marketing matters: a great way of getting attention for your book and at the same time getting some interesting case stories to write about is to post calls for stories on your social media and your emailing list.

When quoting or referencing people, if it's a short quote, a "fair use" quote, you can use it without getting permission. The books you write should never need permission because they're books about your IP, not someone else's IP. Collect and write down your references as you go along. Do not leave it till the end because you'll never do it, you will forget things and it will turn into a nightmare which means the book won't get finished.

Out of the ego chamber

There are two steps that will determine whether your book is a sloppy shelf-sitter, wasting book space or flying off the shelves as the most gifted and referred bestseller.

The problem is most authors don't like this stage.

It's all about advice – accepting it!

And we're too used to giving it.

**Beta readers (and bringing your Book Lovers Team
closer) and a professional edit (which we look at in the
next chapter) will blast you unceremoniously out of your
comfy corner.**

You need at least a second pair of eyes. You might need
three or four or five pairs of eyes. I advise against too
many pairs of eyes because then you are in, what I call,
"the herding cats game". You send your manuscript out
to three beta readers. One of them comes back; the other
two go off on a holiday. And now you feel like you've got to
wait for those two to come back in – you are herding cats.
It becomes a mess.

Select a small number of beta readers from your Book
Lovers Team, at least two, no more than five. Choose
carefully. There's a tendency at this stage to send your
book to people who love you, so that you don't get harsh
criticism. Resist!

Not all beta readers are created equal:

- Who they are. They need to have a good grasp of the
  written language. They need to be able to tell you
  if something reads wrong or is uncomfortable. Your
  mom might be the best beta reader, but she probably
  isn't.

- They must *want* to do the beta read. Don't coerce
  anybody.

- They need to have the time available. You need to give them a timescale (feedback in a week, please) and if they don't have that time available, then they're not right for your beta read, unless you can change the deadline.

- Are they "like" your target market? We started thinking about the one person who you are writing this book for. Now you can start widening to think about who else is like "Jane" or "John". Who else really should read your book? It's better if your beta readers are a little bit like the target market that you've selected.

- If you selected menopausal women as your reader avatar, probably your best beta reader is not a guy (unless they've got a wife, a female friend, or a mother that has gone through the same experience). It just won't resonate with them. They'll be giving you a different type of read.

- They must have your best interests at heart (no hidden agendas).

- They have to be competent and confident enough to give real feedback. There's a level of self-assurance that people need in order to be able to give that feedback.

- If you're on a programme with me, then other people on the cohort could help out here (reciprocate or barter with them).

What is a beta read?

We have to instruct our beta readers on what we want from them. Their job is not to fix the problems. They don't have to do an edit, be grammar police nor fix typos; they don't have to fix punctuation, spelling nor put all the commas in. **They're not copy editors – you pay for that.**

Your wonderful beta readers just have to spot the logical problems and tell you what they like and don't like. They're reading it as a reader, not as a copy editor.

You can get some sample beta reader questions in
Book Lovers Team Dashboard:
www.ShortValuableBooks.com

There are some very specific things I want you to ask your beta readers to do. You can change the formatting of these questions and the way you write them, depending on your book and who you're asking.

1. **Read through quickly.** They should be able to get through a 20,000 word book in less than two hours. You want them to read it quickly because you don't want them to go into the details of editing, grammar, punctuation and spelling.

2. **Highlight anything weird.** They're looking for outliers,

things that are confusing or repeated, jumps from one idea to another without being clear.

3. **Note when they get bored (page #)**. What page did they stop reading? What page didn't have any value? If there are five pages in your book where beta readers said it was too boring, then you can go and fix them. Add value to those pages.

4. **Look for the value per page**. Were the excited and surprised by how valuable your book was?

5. **Spot the IP.** Could they see your special way of explaining complex things?

6. **Is the table of contents interesting?** Did you want to read the book? What were the most interesting bits?

7. **Have you dropped credibility clues?** Don't dump all the credibility clues into your author bio at the end or the introduction (which we don't call the introduction).

It's no good getting all this feedback if you don't do something with it.

Take note of all the feedback, decide what *you* think, accept or reject their ideas and incorporate it into your main manuscript. Then you'll be ready to do a self-edit.

Watch the video about how to do a self-edit of your
manuscript: www.ShortValuableBooks.com

A quick note on self-editing (go and watch the video for
"how" to do it):

- Look for vagaries and maybes – you are the authority,
be confident so the reader can be confident: change
from A Model to "**The** Model...", phrase as a confident
"**How** to...", be assertive with "**Replaces** the..."

- Search for your filler words – we all have them – our
verbal tics. Mine is "stuff". When I'm writing quickly
(and being lazy), I'll drop stuffs all over the place.

- You cannot self-edit well in the same place you wrote.
Change the environment.

There's a side effect of writing your book: you have to
articulate your current thinking. It forces you to nail down
one idea, and live with it. It takes you out of chaos (all your
ideas), through constraints (one framework or system)
and into creation (one book).

It's easy to get caught up in writing too much, spending
years on research, editing and re-editing, navel-gazing,
changing direction and starting again.

Gareth Helm, author of *The Marketing Leader's Code*,

noted: *"I found having my core framework, that I'd articulated for my book, and bringing it with me into my business day meant I kept getting more collateral. As I related my working life to the book, talked to clients, helped them get their results I created more ideas. It became more real and current."*

You've now had your first external eyes read your book, you've stopped crying, made the changes and you're feeling quite satisfied with your work. Time to send it off to publishers and wait for the bidding war?

Notes

1. For one client, "statistical analysis" got transcribed to "sisters testicle analysis".

2. You can read more about how falling off a horse helped me write more here: https://theassetpath.com/tap7-commit-to-action/three-handstands-habit/

3. Jonathan Gottschall, *The Storytelling Animal: How Stories Make Us Human*, Harper Collins Publishers, 2013

6.

IT'S ABOUT SELECTING YOURSELF, NOT WAITING TO BE SELECTED (AGAIN) – YOU HAVE PUBLISHING OPTIONS

We've been sold a story that only traditionally published books give us the credibility clues, the ego boost and the acclaim that we crave. Now you know that isn't so! But, self-publishing has a bad name: it's for romance, self-help and vampire fiction writers. Vanity presses are rip-offs for your uncle's autobiography. If you self-publish, it will look dreadful and people will know you couldn't get a publishing deal. Hybrid is really expensive and you still lose royalties, and traditional publishing you only do for the credibility ...

How do you get your book published, ensure it looks great and you keep the royalties and control?

Your options – self, hybrid, traditional, cohort

It's worth deciding what publishing route you're going to select upfront because they have different challenges and issues, and you have to do things in the right order. In addition, your choice will impact (financially and technically) how you can use your book in your business.

Traditional publishing

Getting published by Bloomsbury or Penguin is one of the most common desires I hear from smart business owners, consultants and coaches. The kudos from being chosen by a major publishing house will improve their reputation, sell books, get them gigs, right? Maybe. It's my experience that the only people who are interested in who published your book are other wannabe authors looking for a publisher. Most readers are interested in the content, not the kudos. Of course, you can use the name of the publisher to help with your marketing. It is a credibility clue – just not as magnificent as people think.

Who makes the decision: They do. You need an agent and a book pitch. You can submit to some traditional publishers online, or through your own contacts and research. A great resource (if you can bear the 1990s vibe) is Publishers Marketplace. I've helped plenty of authors write their book pitch; we've spent weeks (sometimes months) getting it just right. We've had some wonderful successes (Bloomsbury, BIS, Taylor and Francis, Pearson). And plenty of disappointments.

It's like the X Factor. There are only so many slots per season (books). You're up against a crowd of hopefuls and some are amazing but the vast majority are pub singers. The judges (commissioning editors) are humans who might be having a bad day, have already seen twenty Taylor Swift soundalikes, have too many submissions to wade through and are not arsed enough.

Really, if you get turned down (especially as a first-time author) by a major publishing house, it's not you, it's the legacy publishing system.

How much it costs: Your biggest expenses are time and emotions. The time cost is real. There's the time writing the pitch and waiting for responses, your time writing the book, and the time it takes to get through their publishing machine (see the point below). These are all opportunity costs – you could be writing the book not the pitch, marketing the book and getting clients instead of waiting for publication.

How much you make (royalties): The myth is you'll make a great advance, earn it back within the first week of publishing and then live off the royalties for the rest of your life, leaving a legacy for your grandchildren.

The truth is most authors don't earn out their advance – if they even get one. Your royalties will be between seven per cent and fifteen per cent depending on the publisher and how good your agent was at negotiating. Remember, they take a cut too – they're not speccing you out for love.

Who's in control: The (robots) publisher. If they can be bothered. Recently I've noticed a diminishing interest in editorial input, a reduction in conversation with my authors and a lack of interest in, well, just about everything to do with your book. It's outsourced, managed, automated. I get it, they have a business to run too. They're working on a blockbuster strategy: one to five per cent of the books they publish will turn into a blockbuster. They have no idea which ones (unless you are famous), so they do just enough to get every book over the line – then place all their bets on whoever is nosing ahead. It could be you (lottery advert in-joke).

Who does the work: You, of course. You have to write the book – that's the biggest job. You also have to get beta readers, handle feedback, rework the edit and proofread. And you have to do the vast majority of the marketing. The publisher will handle the editing (if you're lucky you'll get constructive editorial input upfront and during your writing, if not you'll get a copy edit), typesetting, cover design and distribution. You do the rest.

How long till your book is on the shelves: Seventeen years. Seriously, between twelve months and two years. Publishers have a schedule, they have a pipeline of books, and a workflow. Get in the queue.

The process: Think of a great book idea, find an agent, sell the idea to the agent, write a book pitch, sell book pitch to the publisher, get feedback from the publisher, and write to their deadline. Then the usual editing, proofing and production.

During book coaching with Ann Latham, The Queen of Clarity, we realised the genius of Ann's ideas and methodology. I knew she had a great shot at getting a publishing deal. We worked on a proposal for publishers that would identify Ann's unique ideas, and demonstrate her platform and previous publishing credentials (Ann's previous books were a huge asset). Ann had two offers from major publishers. She selected Bloomsbury, who would go on to publish *The Power of Clarity* as their number one business book for 2021. Ann's next book (number 6) was published under the Intellectual Perspective Press banner in 2022.

For some people getting traditionally published is the right choice. You will need to craft a great pitch. Download your own copy of a book pitch for agents and The Publisher's Canvas.
www.ShortValuableBooks.com

Hybrid publishing

Do not underestimate the benefits of a hybrid publisher. The best ones (I can recommend a few) take great care to select authors who will benefit from writing a book. They give feedback on your manuscript and recommend solutions (not only the things they sell). The problem is most hybrid publishers are vanity publishers in posh frocks.

Assuming you haven't been duped by a vanity press (you pay, they publish) and you are working with a good hybrid publisher (they turn manuscripts down if they're not good enough), then this is what you can expect.

Who makes the decision: Depends. Probably you about the direction of your book. Probably them about editorial and design.

How much it costs: A lot. From $7,500 upwards.

How much you make (royalties): You should be looking for at least 25% royalties (after costs) to you. I would expect 50% from a hybrid publisher.

Who's in control: You are paying, but they are in control. They have a process, systems, methodologies and standards (hopefully!). You will be expected to fit into their system and they will take on the headache of project managing your book.

Who does the work: Like in traditional publishing deals you are up for the vast majority of the effort. Many hybrid publishers will also offer a "write for you" service – ghostwriting – at an extra cost. Your hybrid publisher will do the edit, interior, cover and get your book into distribution. Some hybrids will advise on marketing and PR (usually an extra service).

How long till your book is on the shelves: They will have a working pipeline of books going through the stages, it can take anywhere from three months (fastest) to about one year to get your book from manuscript to shelf. A definite saving from traditional publishing.

The process: Think of a great book idea and write it, find a good hybrid publisher, agree terms and pay an upfront fee and submit manuscript to an agreed deadline. Then the usual editing, proofing, production.

Self-publishing

Self-publishing gets a really bad name. Like self-dentistry! Who in their right mind would do it? Smart business owners and leaders, that's who. When you know how to get your book self-published, make sure it looks professional, know who to use (you don't do it all *yourself*!), and have a simplified process and plan, self-publishing is a good choice.

Who makes the decision: You! You choose you, and all the experts and professionals to get the book finished and out there. If you have a great idea, a business outcome and strategy for your book, and the energy to pull all the pieces together, then you can decide to self-publish.

How much it costs: A lot of your time, especially if you are managing the process yourself. Budget for at least $3,000 depending on word count, and how much messing about you do (if you dilly dally about the edit, rework the cover seventeen times, and change the subtitle at the last minute, then be prepared to pay more).

How much you make (royalties): Here's the best bit – one hundred per cent. Not only that but you get to decide if you give books away, do deals and discounts and make special editions. All of these options impact how much you will make from your book. Your marketing efforts are stymied with the other publishing methods (you have a "partner" to appease, and pay).

Who's in control: You, you lovely little control freak.

Who does the work: You and a select team of professionals. If you think self-publishing means you do it all yourself you will probably end up making a dreadful book, that's badly thought through, is unreadable and looks like the cast-offs from a 1970s pimp's wardrobe. You need a team.

How long till your book is on the shelves: Depends on you and your trusty team of pros. Assume about three months from final manuscript to shelf.

The process: Think of a good book idea, test it and write it. Select your team of professionals (at least one editor and designer), manage the editing and design process and publish it on Amazon and IngramSpark. Collect your money.

Cohort Publishing

Of course, there's an alternative – Intellectual Press Publishing – for very special people. You get elite coaching through a proven framework, with inbuilt co-marketing, accountability and support. I only accept the top tier thinkers. Publishing is professional, free and guaranteed if you follow the system. But you have to meet the demanding criteria: atomic idea, beta read, to timescale and co-marketing all designed to get your book read. Oh, and you earn all the royalties (there's an opt-in, trust-based reverse royalties scheme). The best of hybrid and self-publishing! Pop me a message if you want to know more.

> Try the Business Book Advisor Diagnostic: What publishing method is right for you? Find out where to spend your time and energy.
> www.ShortValuableBooks.com

Explore your opportunities, allocate resources and commit to action – see The Asset Path in chapter 1.

Whatever route you take you are up for most of the marketing. So build it into the process, make a book that is searchable (one real person with a problem you can solve) and shareable (so valuable people talk about it and refer it).

The non-negotiables

Irrespective of your route to shelf – there are a few non-negotiables:

1. Beta readers (which we covered in the last chapter)

2. The best editor you can afford

3. Prototype your book, and socialise it a bit!

The best editor

When you've had your fill of feedback from the amateurs (the bloody marvellous beta readers who deserve medals, chocolates and flowers), and you've done your self-edit (and made yourself completely bored of your own book), you'll need to find a great editor.

When you find one, keep them.

There are plenty of places online to find editors (try Reedsy), but I enthusiastically suggest you ask for a referral or recommendation from colleagues or friends who have written a book you admire.

If you are going the traditional or hybrid publishing routes, your editor should be part of the package. That means you don't get to choose. Don't keep them at arm's length, throw them your book and wait for the red penning. Get on a call, explain your book, tell them what you're worried about, and get them invested in your book before they get their red pen out.

If you are lucky enough to select your own editor, check out a few books they've edited, speak to a couple of their authors, have a chat with them and check out their methodology. Assuming they know their 'I's from their T's', the most important concern is if you can get on with them. They are going to be critiquing your "baby" that you've been working on for the last six months. Are they kind, firm, thorough? Do they appreciate the pain an author goes through?

I have worked with editors and publishers who have built up their authors, helped them make their books brilliant, and worked harmoniously with them to create something even better. I have also worked with "school marms", who wield their red pens (metaphorically, remember we're in the twenty-first century) ready to do battle with their author, demonstrate their dominance and draw blood.

Lisa de Caux, our editor at Intellectual Perspective Press: *"I'm part of the author's book team and that means respecting and understanding the author's voice and their context. Consistency is key for me: internal consistency within the book and, for Intellectual Perspective Press, consistency across the series."*

There are two types of edit you should be interested in if you choose you. (If you are being published you don't get much choice and you'll probably only get a copy edit):

1. Developmental edit: To help you work out the big issues, fix structure, check that you've included everything. As you've been working through the process in this book you may not need a developmental edit (and if you did you would have noticed earlier because your beta readers would have made it very clear).

You will need a copy edit.

2. Copy edit: Only go to copy edit when you are finished writing, beta reading and self-editing. When *you* are satisfied with your manuscript. Your copy editor will meticulously check for spelling, grammar and punctuation errors.

Your editor is your last line of defence. Make sure they're on your side.

You may also select a proof edit at typeset stage, after the interior design has been completed.

Prototype your book, and socialise it a bit!

The problem with going the traditional or hybrid publishing routes is that you have to fit into their program of publishing and production. These days that does not include a pre-production prototype phase, where you get hands and eyes on a printed copy of your book.

If you choose yourself and go for self-publish (or cohort publishing with me) you can schedule in time for a printed prototype proof. After your book has been designed get print on demand prototypes delivered. Prototyping your book is circle 5 in The Asset Path (from Chapter 1) – it's a vital step, at the heart of the path.

Prototyping your book:

- Helps you spot the errors that have slipped through – the missing commas, the overlooked diagram names, the truncated footnotes. It doesn't matter how good you are, even the big name publishers let the odd error through.

- Gives you have a marketing opportunity – photos of your book, send one to your lovely BLTers making them feel even more special, pop a copy in the post to your favourite client. Always be marketing!

- Provides another chance for feedback – did you miss something? It's much easier to spot in a printed prototype. The very act of seeing it in a different medium helps you 'look' at it differently!

- Makes it easier to get reviews (you can also use ARCs, see chapter 7).

A printed proof is a non-negotiable for me.

The marketing breaker or maker

Remember back in chapter 4, the most important things that will get your book picked up and read? Well, number one was your cover.

Your cover is more than a pretty picture with a few words. It's the feeling the book will give a potential reader. Is it serious or light-hearted, detailed or big picture, academic or actionable, standout or blend in, exciting or stable, professional or not?

Your book will be judged by its cover.

Make sure it's judged fairly and accurately.

> **Marketing matters:** You'll find a lot of people put three or four covers out on social media and ask for favourites. This is a great way to get feedback, attention and interest in your book. You won't always get qualified *design* advice though!

Even with a traditional publisher you should get some input on the cover design. Of course your book might be part of a series, and have constraints on the design, but your input will be encouraged.

It's not just the front; books have big behinds too. Your

back cover blurb (which will also probably appear in the book description on Amazon and other retailers) will help a reader make a decision – buy and read, or not. You might add a credibility clue or two – endorsements from well-known people help with the buying decision-making process.

You don't need to stick with conventions. One of my Map-type books has nine beautiful images on the back cover. The images tell the story of the book.

Writing the back cover blurb is an art. Do not leave it to the publisher – it's your responsibility. It's your chance to sell the book. One way is to use the SCQ methodology to write an enticing first paragraph, then bullet the benefits of your book. Or you could just make a shocking, against-type controversial statement. Perhaps include your main model. Revisit your lexicon. What can you use?

Do not leave it to chance, nor the last minute.

Test your back cover blurb with your BLT. Test your front cover with your market.

So, you've made it this far. You have a book in your hands that's been tested with your beta readers, edited by professionals, produced by experts. People will be flocking to buy it, right?

Please take 5 minutes to leave me a review, it helps other people to decide if they want to read the book, and I'll be eternally grateful. If you're reading on Kindle just scroll to the end of the book. If you're reading the paperback, please go to your favourite bookstore.

Remember, you can get the promised downloads at www.shortvaluablebooks.com or scan the QR code.

7.

IT'S ABOUT VALUE NOT MARKETING – STOP MAKING NOISE, LISTEN FOR SIGNAL

You've written your book, it's great, people love it and you've been getting reviews. Now what? Write another book? (You masochist!) You could just get addicted to writing books – I have. But what about those lovely people who don't read books? Or your clients who have read all your books and are still looking for more from you? Your superfans, your dedicated "expects" and referrers want more. People are busy doing their stuff. Running businesses, caring for families and tiktoking. You are not only competing for their attention from your competitors, but from overwhelm, exhaustion, complacency and cat videos.

How do you create more assets to serve your growing audience, keep bringing new people in, and make enough "noise" to break through the cacophony?

Your book needs to be so brilliant it markets itself.

Marketing matters: Harry from marketingexamples.com says that content is discovered in one of two ways: people **search** for it or people **share** it. Your job with your book is to hit the sweet spot – it needs to be **shareable**, referable and so bloody good people can't stop talking about it; and it needs to be discoverable because people will actively **search** to fix the problem you are solving.

Over a hundred years ago, John Wanamaker, the forefather of marketing, allegedly said: *"Half the money I spend on advertising is wasted; the trouble is I don't know which half."*[1] Twenty-five years ago I turned it into a joke that I'd share on stages around the UK: fifty per cent of your marketing works and fifty per cent doesn't, the trick is knowing which is which. Now, I'd say ninety per cent doesn't work and ten per cent does – and yet we spend all our time on the visible, pretend marketing, not waving at lovely readers, but drowning in a sea of sameness.[2]

There are at least 1,763 things you could do to market your book. Some of them will work. Do those.

What's in the ten per cent?

You've done these:

- Be clear on what job your book has to do for your business (chapter 1)

- Solve a problem for one real reader/buyer (chapter 2)

- Be referable to get word of mouth, and pass the Tube test (chapter 2)

- Make it so valuable people won't stop talking about it (chapters 3 & 6)

And next:

- Be visible where "they" are (suspects, prospects, expects, referrers)

- Use other people's time, money, and platform (social, guesting, partnership)

- Get to "owned" as quickly as possible (build that list)

- Then reuse, recycle, upcycle (because one book is never enough)

The M Word – set your marketing direction

You've done the clever bit, which is break the brain world barrier. You've actually got something out of your brain and turned it into something that other people can see. You've written the book. Now what? At this stage newly-authored business owners often fall into one of two thinking traps:

1. Write it and they will come, or

2. Nobody wants to hear about my book, again!

The second trap occurs due to a lack of a marketing plan coupled with a dash of naivety. The first comes from assuming you are the centre of the universe! Both traps mean your book won't be doing the job it is designed for – demonstrating your authority to the correct audience!

Marketing is telling the right people about the thing that's good for them. **Creating it is beautiful, but shipping and sharing is how you change the world and how everyone benefits.**

Every chapter and step of the way we've had an outcome we've been working towards. Understanding our reader, crafting an outline, and writing the first draft. These outcomes were atomic – we could know when we were done.

Our outcome in this chapter is **a marketing direction, not a marketing disaster.**

In the olden days (!) the barrier to "marketing" your product, service or idea, was an actual product, service or idea (let's start with the basics!), a designer, someone who could string words together, a place to do the "marketing" such as a periodical, etc, a blank cheque and you were set to go... Now the barrier to entry is a Canva account, and, if you want to get fancy, Jarvis.ai. This means it's so much harder and so much easier.

Go back to chapter 1. What job will your book do for you and your business? You decided where your book would work, and what it would do. Your marketing direction needs to be focused on achieving these jobs.

STAGES OF COMMUNICATION

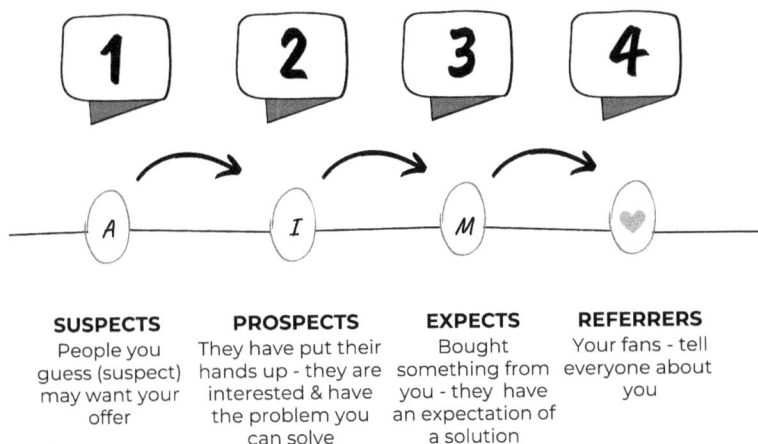

1	**2**	**3**	**4**
A	I	M	♥
SUSPECTS	**PROSPECTS**	**EXPECTS**	**REFERRERS**
People you guess (suspect) may want your offer	They have put their hands up - they are interested & have the problem you can solve	Bought something from you - they have an expectation of a solution	Your fans - tell everyone about you

If you want your book to generate leads (suspect to prospect) for your consultancy business, you may have decided to give your book to people for free (if they qualify), and to use it to educate them about your more expensive program (turn them into expects). Your book may be the first sale, taking prospects to expects. Or it may be the best way of reminding your current clients to refer you, or to get speaking gigs, or to be a corporate gift, or ...

If you just wait, hoping people will buy it, you will have

wasted the investment that you made in your own time, and any costs that you've had to produce your book. Remember, your book has a job to do.

Download the Seven Book Job Recipes (includes free plus shipping, free ebook, low cost, low cost and upsell, gateway, partner and sponsor) if you're still not sure. www.ShortValuableBooks.com

Your marketing activities will be determined by the job your book has to do. Here are twelve activities that could work for all jobs, split by timescale.

During writing:

1. **Select a social channel and get visible:** go where your one reader hangs out with other people like them. If that's on LinkedIn, get visible there. Think about what your potential readers need to understand to make reading your book an obvious decision. Focus on why-to and simple how-to type content. Make a spreadsheet with ideas you need to share (they will probably already be in your book). Batch writing posts. Post daily. Engage with everybody who responds.

2. **Book Lovers Team:** send them advanced readers copies before you go wild and launch. ARCs, if you'd like to use the cool term, are sent for a reason. You're giving them out to get reviews. You need reviews on

Amazon, and your BLTers are your best starting place. ARCs are finalised production-ready printed copies of your book, unlike prototypes as discussed in the previous chapter.

3. **Start a mailing list:** if you don't have a mailing list, or you haven't messaged in a while, now is the time to "own" your method of communicating with people. Get them off the socials, out of the groups and into your mailing list. Good options are Mailchimp, Substack and Ghost.

Launch:

1. **Offers for buying in launch week:** make it worthwhile to buy your book in the first week, this will give you a boost in the bestseller lists, and you might just get a category bestseller status. What can you give away to the first 100 buyers? What happens if people buy more than five books? What are you going to offer your first five readers?

2. **Promotional pricing:** Amazon encourages ebook deals and promotions. You can run these in any 90-day session that you're enrolled in KDP Select,[3] you can do an ebook deal, a countdown deal or a free book deal. A free ebook promotion in the first thirty days will help get reviews.

3. **Double up on social, shared and owned:** Send a lot of messages to your list. They're already in your

communication stages – gone from suspects to at least prospects. They should be interested in your book. Share book excerpts, tell them about the offers and promotional pricing. Ask your mates (remember them?) to buy, share it on their socials and share it to their mailing lists.

You can read my The Amazon Bestseller Plan[4] book if you want more details about doing a bestseller launch (and the work involved).
www.ShortValuableBooks.com

Estelle Read's book, *Inner Brilliance: Outer Shine*, got bestseller status. Estelle says: "*My publisher tried to manage my expectations by telling me my book wouldn't be a bestseller.*"

There are 48.5 million books on Amazon. When her book was pre-released in December, it was #708,752. In the first week of sales, while Estelle was on holiday it steadily climbed to the #1 spot under "Hot new releases". "*I don't think I've ever been hot in my life, (other than being perimenopausal). I was more than satisfied with this result. As I scrolled to the bottom of my book page it was like I'd been winded. I doubled up with glee when I saw it was at #6,729. This might not sound like a win; however, it had become an Amazon bestseller in three categories.*"

Post launch:

1. **Ask for reviews:** You will have to do this a lot. You want people to read your book. When they have, ask them for a review. People are busy, remind them! Ask fellow authors. They know how much effort went into writing the book, and they are much more open to reviewing, because they've been there too.

2. **Serialise ideas (not the book):** You have captured and organised your ideas, now is the time to share them (again) in bite size chunks. Every time you do, put a call to buy your book at the end.

3. **Get on the road:** well, podcasts and interviews at least. Podcasts tell people you're special, you've been selected. People hear you talking about your idea and the book. It's great for connecting, building relationships and credibility clueing.

You have created a vault of value during the process of writing your book. When Andy Bass, a long-time client of mine, launched his book, *Start With What Works*[5] *in 2021, we realised he could put some of those assets to better use. We made ebooks, worksheets and presentation decks: assets that can be remixed and reused for future marketing and social media needs, that would encourage buyers, reward readers and interest his target market to get in touch with him.* **We turned his book into his brand.**

Forever and ever:

1. **Dominate one social channel:** Share excerpts of valuable bits (your whole book is valuable, but you know what I mean). Share your one-liners and phrases you want to be known for (from your lexicon). Share cases from the book; tag the people. Share your system, model or IP as an image. Share testimonials and reviews of the book.

2. **Tell your story to get coverage, partnerships and PR:** create contacts and partnerships with magazines that are specific to your target market. Start local or niche. If you've moved to Spain, and you're a Birmingham girl, you could maybe get some PR for your book about Spain on the Birmingham Post. Or, if you've written a book for accountants, start with the financial magazines and groups.

3. **Add value, always:** by using your book as a credibility clue. Offer free chapters (your best chapters) for people who sign up to your newsletter; write a special chapter just for readers that adds to the story and builds more value. Make a video about the book and explain your system, model or IP. Create a workbook and offer the PDF version for free. (People who get the free workbook will really want to buy the whole book or even maybe "buy" the author!)

One of my clients runs a training company, training people how to sell cars for all of the big manufacturers. He wrote a book, made a deal with one of the big magazines in his industry, who gave his book away with their magazine, and paid him for the privilege. It can be just as easy to sell one hundred books as it is to sell one.

Marketing advice that might stop you from going bonkers

Should you do a launch?

Should you do podcasts?

Should you try for an Amazon bestseller?

All these shoulds … You don't have to do everything, but you do have to do something.

You must execute, take action, break the brain / world barrier and tell people about it.

1. **Think in campaigns (sprints not marathons):** Create short organised campaigns. Select one or two marketing tactics, not all of them all at once, that you feel comfortable doing and, with a little bit of help, you can get done. Create your campaign-driven marketing plans as a spreadsheet, a series of Post-it notes on your wall or a serious Gantt chart in notion.so. You can do it however you want, but have a plan.

2. **Assign Responsibilities (not just you):** You've put all this effort into writing the book and creating the book.

You've invested time and money. Now is not the time to step back and wait for things to happen. You may need to get help; you may need to assign responsibilities. Ask partners, friends and colleagues to be involved, keep your Book Lovers Team on the inside. Allocate resources (circle 4 in The Asset Path).

3. **Constraints are good for you. Boundaries are essential:** You could do all 1,763 marketing things for your book, and work only on marketing for the next six months, and you still may have not done all of the possible marketing things. So you have to make decisions; you have to put constraints in place. How much time, money and energy will you spend? You should also consider what you want to do, what you love doing, what you won't do, who you want to work with and who you want to partner with.

4. **Start in your comfort zone:** Many of the marketing tasks you could do may be really far outside your comfort zone. Rather than throw yourself outside your comfort zone and feel really uncomfortable, I suggest that you start by getting uncomfortable in your comfort zone. With all of those tactics that you *could* do, what are the ones that while they might feel uncomfortable, you are most likely to actually do?

5. **The only good marketing plan is one that you actually do:** Think about what things you will actually do rather than all the things you could do. Be constrained, within your comfort zone, but push the

edges of your comfort zone so that eventually you'll just pop out.

6. **Use all your assets:** You've got at least three assets: the PDF of the final book, the physical book, and a Kindle/Ebook. Each asset will attract different readers. You also have your book cover, reviews, your images and models. Exploit your IP (this is circle 8 on The Asset Path).

7. **Cultivate relationships with influencers:** And I don't mean the Facebook pouty type influencers and the Instagrammers (though, if that's right for your target market, then you can). I mean influencers, the people who can give you access to their market.

Marketing means sharing the value with the people who need it, which means you need some collateral to do the marketing.

Basic marketing collateral:

1. **An up-to-date author image:** a professional-looking author shot that gives you credibility.

2. **3D book covers:** are as cheap as chips.

3. **A website or landing page for your book:** keep it simple, a one pager, use software like Carrd.co for less than $50 per year.

4. **Book banners:** for your website, socials, LinkedIn, for your web pages and for marketing in general.

5. **Amazon Author Central:** add your details and the RSS feed to your blog, videos and your bio. You can claim all your books under one account.

6. **Amazon A+:** Amazon A+ is now open to small publishers and self-publishers. If you've been traditionally published you will need to ask your publisher to add these images. Use all the real estate Amazon provides to sell your book.

7. **Reviews:** don't only focus on Amazon: get reviews on LinkedIn, your website, etc.

8. **Affiliate account:** set up an affiliate account on Amazon, you will make a small extra royalty for selling your book.

Don't wait and hope that people will buy your book. This last stage – marketing – is the most important. It's why we've been talking about it all the way through the book. Don't let your ego get in the way, your fear stop you from stepping up, or 'no's stop you from getting to 'yes'. Look back to the plans you made at the beginning when you never thought you'd even get this far. Look at how far you've come. Well done you!

One book is never enough – think upcycle series-ly

To get a book in your hands we've gone through the chaos → constraints → creation process. We delved into the chaos, thought about our one reader, and did the research. We constrained that chaos, made decisions, selected an atomic idea and made an outline. Then we decided what we were going to write, we wrote it and we got feedback. You created assets for your business that are aligned with your business outcomes. **You did the hard work of making something that broke the brain ⚡ world barrier.**

Any time you create something, you're going to cause some new chaos. People will ask for the audio book, more worksheets, downloads, videos, a podcast ... Your creation will create chaos, and your responsibility, your role and job over the lifetime of your business, is to manage this chaos, constraints, creation process.

You get feedback from the market when you ship and share. Now, how are you going to serve that demand?

Remember your TLCs, the Thought Leadership Canvasses? The great thing about the TLC is you can use it for all your marketing and business asset decisions: create a few relatable stories and case stories, describe your processes and then mix and match for each communication. It's plug and play, not one size fits all.

Avoid these mistakes with claiming your IP (these are circles 7, 8 and 9 on The Asset Path from Chapter 1**):**

1. **Not leveraging your assets:** Even experienced people who have published a book, developed a programme or created a system fail to reuse, recycle and upcycle their investment. To amplify your credibility, attract more clients and get a seat at the table, use your assets. It's not enough to "create it and hope", you must make the most of your IP, quickly and frequently.

2. **Not packaging and selling your sawdust:** Your thinking and creative process, the way you've developed your products and services and written your book, and the investment you've made in your learning are all potential assets. Your sawdust is probably more valuable than most people's IP. It's time to sell your sawdust!

3. **Not exploiting your "old" ideas, products, IP:** Really successful consultants, trainers and thought leaders make sure they package their learning after every engagement. That's how they productise and capitalise on their ideas and IP, instead of racing off to the next job. You have a resource exploitation opportunity. Work out what's the best asset to explore and exploit right now, so you don't waste your precious time and resources.

4. **Only providing an idea in one delivery mode:** You can upcycle your IP in multiple different delivery modes. Your podcast can be turned into articles. Your articles can transform into a book. Your book can become your best salesperson. Videos and audios can be remodelled into a course or series, into a membership site or paid subscription. Your printed book can become an audio book.

5. **Writing only one book:** Write another book (series-ly). Don't consider a book a one-off legacy-type experience. There are massive benefits to writing more books: you can develop your ideas, delve deeper, speak to a different reader, share new ideas, respond to new technologies or techniques etc. Amazon also rewards series of books by showing them together – if a reader buys one book in your series, they will see the other books and might even buy them.

Do what Albert does: I have bought (and read!) all of Albert's books. I'm his number one fan (not in a scary Misery-type way![6]). If you're into constraints, systems thinking and mental models, then you might have heard of Albert Rutherford. If you look him up on Amazon you will find he writes short, valuable, atomic books. Lots of them. If he had written one big book covering all these topics he might have been able to sell it for thirty dollars. I have bought all his short books, and spent at least sixty dollars. He's doubled his income from me, and more importantly, I prefer these bitesize ideas that I can read in one sitting.

1. **Create a chain of atomic ideas** (think back to the TikTok devourers), delivered in multiple modes (book, audio, ebook, course, webinar, workshop, etc.) to different people, one person at a time.

2. **Then bundle your books**, ideas, courses, models (assets) into more valuable assets that demand a higher price.

I could have written a 50,000 word book on my method for writing books but you would still be reading in a week's time. Reading isn't going to get your book written, you need to write, you need to get feedback. I have made you a shed load of extra resources to help with the process, and there will be more books, but they'll all be short.

Don't let other people summarise your book and get better sales than you. Sites like Blinkist.com, GetAbstract.com and SparkNotes are excellent for your research as a reader, but bad for your pocket as writer. Don't let people curate your content, curate it yourself! Atomic baby!

You probably won't get rich from one book, but you might just get read, understood and selected.

Notes

1. As always there's some doubt who said it,
   https://www.marketingsociety.com/the-library/why-
   it%E2%80%99s-time-say-goodbye-ikthtmisoaiw – for our
   purposes it really doesn't matter!

2. Stevie Smith, "Not Waving but Drowning" from Collected
   Poems of Stevie Smith. Copyright © 1972, New Directions
   Publishing Corporation.

3. KDP Select is Amazon's way of keeping you in their clutches.
   I have a love/hate relationship with Amazon. Use the
   advantages to your advantage, and be aware of the
   downside.

4. The Amazon Bestseller Plan: How To Make Your Book An
   Amazon Bestseller in 24 Hour or Less, Joe Gregory and
   Debbie Jenkins, Lean Marketing Press, 2006

5. Andy Bass PhD, *Start With What Works: A faster way to
   grow your business,* Pearson Business, 2021. Read more
   about how we worked together here:
   https://theassetpath.com/case-story-andy-wins-a-
   publishing-deal-with-a-major-publisher-and-needs-
   marketing-assets/

6. Steven King's book, Misery, tainted my childhood dreams of
   being a writer.

8.

SHORT VALUABLE BOOKS: THE BEST WAY OF HELPING MORE PEOPLE, QUICKLY

The problem with writing – with all "thinking" disciplines – is that you can be doing this forever.

After more than twenty years of helping clients turn their thoughts into things, studying *The Principles of Scientific Management*,[1] coupled with my engineering background and love of constraints (not that kind!), I have come to the conclusion that the only way to turn your thoughts into things, and get your ideas out into the world is to:

1. Make the **ideas atomic** – the smallest workable unit (a Minimum Valuable Asset)

2. Have a **proven system** that works to produce the "thing" (this book for books)

3. Set a **constraint** – time, money, resources – and be accountable to the constraint

4. **Iterate** and improve yourself, as well as the process.

Many people don't get their ideas turned into things (books written) because they skip an element in the process, reinvent the process or don't even have a process to start with.

Now you have the process you can turn your thoughts into many different things. You just need to find the right specialist to give you the blueprint.

There are only two real mistakes when writing a book:

1. Not starting

2. Not finishing

You've got to get started and you've got to go all the way.

Not starting can be solved by:

- Knowing your book's job and how it will grow relationships and your business

- Deeply understanding and caring for your one reader and aligning your Most Wanted Response with theirs

- Deciding on the correct type of book (Directions, Map, Landmark) which will achieve your objectives and share your intellectual perspective

Not finishing can be solved by:

- Starting with a brilliant outline that has been tested with beta readers

- Writing in whatever mode works best for you and setting yourself up for success with a writing habit

- Getting clear on your publishing options – knowing that your thoughts will turn into a beautiful, useful thing that people want to read

- Understanding that the finish line isn't a book in your hands (though that's pretty cool!), that it's the new start line for your business

If you're smart about it, writing a business book can be one of the best and fastest ways to accelerate your own personal brand and authority.

The benefits of writing a business book are immense. Not only do you get to share your own stories, tips and advice with the world, but it also serves as great proof to support your own personal authority.

Notes

1. It's good, but not terribly sexy for bedtime reading! The Principles of Scientific Management, Frederick Winslow Taylor, Dover Publications, 1997

WHO IS DEBBIE JENKINS?

As a kid, I devoured second hand, thumbed copies of the Bible, Isaac Asimov, the revised 13th edition of Encyclopedia Britannica (except PAS-PLA, missing in action) and the Reader's Digests. I knew I'd end up doing something with books, despite a careers advisor warning me against it.

The first publishing business I started in 2004, specialised in publishing unique non-fiction titles by genuine experts and thought leaders with niche books that, although mainstream publishers tend to overlook, were packed with information hungry readers wanted. At the heart of everything we did was fair play and efficiency. We worked hard to create a virtuous circle and put profit back into our authors' pockets while building a viable business ourselves. I exited that company in 2011, and they've gone on to do even greater things.

I love working with smart consultants, coaches and mentors who are brilliant at serving their clients, *and* also need to take care of their own practice.

I've been running my own consultancy businesses for the last 25+ years. My first business was a digital marketing agency in the '90s helping consultants, coaches, trainers, speakers and expert advisors to grow their business while reducing marketing waste. Over the next 3 years I grew that company to 12 employees, an office in the city, a chillax room for the team... I thought I knew what I was doing. But I missed capitalising on a vital step – I didn't create enough assets that would work for me so that I didn't have to keep on selling my own and my team's time.

I know that it's easy to get caught up delivering to clients, keeping on top of trends and technology, marketing and proposal writing, racing from job to job. It's hard to squeeze in time for your own personal professional development, let alone find space to think about creating assets. And there's the dilemma, **because without these assets you'll always be bouncing from job to job, selling your time not your value, and leaving your best ideas on your busy desk.**

Over the last 25 years I have helped COOs from Microsoft, VPs from McDonald's and Executives from Mars (the company, not the planet) create, build and launch assets that have helped them win clients, build their personal practices and become published authors*. Through my publishing company I published over 80 business books. After I sold it I went on to help more than 30 smart business owners write their legacy book, and coached hundreds of consultants to market themselves, their business, and their IP. I have ghostwritten bestselling business books for venture capitalists, CFOs, MBEs, professors, mentors and coaches. I have designed and marketed apps, produced websites and written/co-written more than 10 books (my first in 2003).

In the last few years, I have had coaching clients get published with Bloomsbury, Pearson, Business Expert Press, BIS, and Taylor & Francis. Other coaching clients chose themselves, decided the best route would be to use a hybrid publisher, or they've self-published. Each route to publishing is valid and has its own pros and cons. Now, I'm helping experts get their book written and published through my own publishing company, Intellectual Perspective Press.

I know how to help you get the clever ideas out of your head (or off your computer) and turned into valuable things (assets) for your business. Assets like business books, whitepapers, converting websites, marketing materials, podcasts ... I also know how to help you use these assets to accelerate your time to impact, achieve visibility and influence, and improve your bottom line – that is The Asset Path.

I have a 1st Class Degree in Electronics Engineering which means I am trained to look for sustainable and innovative solutions to problems, I understand technology and software development, and I can create models and frameworks that people can use (and I know what a MOSFET is). I moved to Southern Spain in 2005. I live at the Disaster Farm (that's not a typo) with a host of animals, where I invite special clients to visit and work on their assets in person. I only work ten months of the year because the Disaster Farm needs my attention too – and if I don't take a break who's going to hand feed the horses juicy carrots and lounge around reading all those books I've bought?

I am determined to help all my clients make the most of their IP, ideas and talent. **I can help you turn your clever ideas into valuable things. And we'll have fun doing it.**

* I work with people from companies that don't start with an M too!

HOW TO TAKE THINGS FURTHER

We can work together one to one. I only take on writing coaching clients who have been referred, are on my contacts list, and I think are a good match. It gets quite personal, it can be cathartic and revelatory, we might discuss things energetically(!) – so we need to be sure I'm the right person to help you.

You can also join my Intellectual Perspective Press inner circle. This is your fastest and easiest way to get ideas out of your head, tested and published as short valuable books, that get read. You will get personal coaching from me, work with a very small group of smart experts, with peer support and advice. But most importantly, you'll get your book out of your head and into the hands of the people who need to read it. This is how we create assets for our business.

Or you can do things at your own pace with Better Than Great sprints. This is an exclusive group of action-oriented consultants and experts who come together to build assets that add value, attract new clients, and make money. This is how we scale The Asset Path.

Get in touch at: www.DebbieJenkins.com

BOOKS YOU COULD READ

I have been informed and educated by a lot of books over the years. Some I re-read frequently, many I refer. Here are just a few of the books you could read to help you stop writing books that nobody reads.

Selling the Invisible: A Field Guide to Modern Marketing by Harry Beckwith, was first published in 1997 and was instrumental in my early business days. My thumbed copy gets referred frequently!

The ONE Thing: The Surprisingly Simple Truth About Extraordinary Results from Gary Keller helped me formulate and stick to the short valuable book idea. You need to write atomic books, that focus on one thing.

Write Useful Books: A modern approach to designing and refining recommendable nonfiction by Rob Fitzpatrick shares many of the same ideas I have been working on with my clients, but he got his book out a year earlier than I did.

Think: Using Pink Sheets to capture and expand your ideas from the Thought Leaders, Matt Church & Peter Cook, is a free ebook that will help you with capture your thoughts. Their philosophy inspired box 4 on my Thought Leadership Canvas.

ACKNOWLEDGEMENTS

Thank you to all my clients over the years who have trusted me with their delicate creations – your confidence in me frequently brings me to tears. I hope I haven't made you cry too many times!

Joe Gregory, my brother, first business partner, friend and most welcome critic – thanks bro!

The Asset Path Professionals: Jayr Cuario, who can turn your ideas into amazing creations – you've taught me the joy of working with a team again; and Lisa de Caux, with her gentle art of editing.

OTHER BOOKS BY DEBBIE JENKINS

Get Debbie's other business books at
www.ShortValuableBooks.com

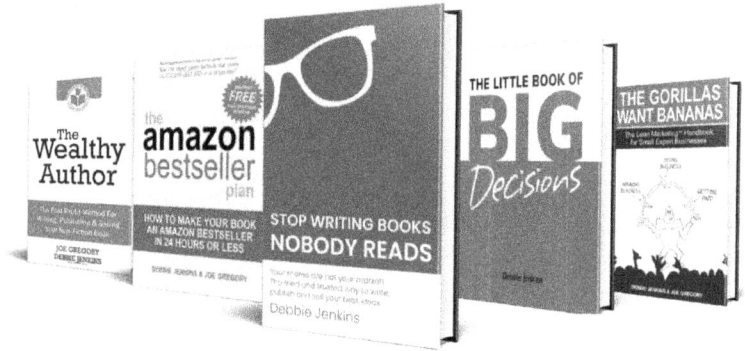

Stop writing books nobody reads is book one in the "Ideas Into Assets" series.

We have *Hacking Serendipity, Stop Starting – Start Stopping* and *The Directions, Map, Landmark Communications Compass for Leaders* coming next.

MORE PRAISE FOR STOP WRITING BOOKS NOBODY READS

I love the book. Jam packed full of value. Really easy to read and her wonderful personality and energy shines through. I could hear her in my head and felt like she was really talking to me. The book has left me feeling that, whilst writing a book that people will read might not be easy, the process can be simple. I am inspired to get started on that process and write my first book.

Susannah Simmons, The Software Adoption Doctor, productivit.co.uk

Stop Writing Books Nobody Reads _is short, sharp and shrewd – a dazzling two-hour crash course in how to get your business book right first time. (Face facts: you're never going to have a second go at it!) Debs Jenkins writes about the realities of publishing with energy, humour and no-nonsense inside knowledge. 'Self-publishing gets a really bad name,' she says. 'Like self-dentistry!' Stop looking in the mirror all the time while you're writing, she advises: you need to break out of 'the ego chamber'. And I loved her advice on how to bring case study stories to life by concentrating on the FFFF formula – firsts, failures, fuck-ups and fightbacks. Douglas 'Hitchhiker's Guide' Adams once wrote that a Sue Lim novel was 'the kind of book that makes you want to sleep with the author'. Debbie's book doesn't go quite that far, but it does make you wish she could be there, squatting on the corner of your desk,_ *chipping in her smart advice and awful warnings, while you write your own business masterpiece.*

Ian Shircore – pro ghostwriter, author of *Conspiracy, NLP and the New Manager* and *So Brightly at the Last: Clive James and the Passion for Poetry*, www.ianshircore.com

Witty, gritty, ruthlessly honest and incredibly helpful, Debs' Jenkins advice in Stop Writing Books Nobody Reads *is worth following because it works. After scribbling thoughts in my notebook for two years and starting to gather them into chapters I joined her first Intellectual Perspectives Press cohort and created* The Slow Coach Approach *in a matter of months. It's getting the good reviews I doubt it would have received had I continued muddling along on my own – and that's because she guided me through researching what my 'one person' needed and shared good practical advice. Debs practices what she preaches by putting huge value on each page.*

Judy Barber, coach, facilitator and author of *The Slow Coach Approach* *www.theslowcoachapproach.com*

Start (and finish!) Debbie Jenkins latest book if you are thinking about writing a business book. Debbie Jenkins provides an informative and entertaining how-to for writing a book that will help you create a book that does the job you need it to do for your business. So-called experts often tell you what to do, but do not actually use their own advice or approach. Debbie Jenkins meta-advice is to provide value on every page of writing. She follows the advice in her book starting with the Table of Contents. She says, "If you can provide value in a table of contents, then the read will be confident you're going to provide in the book." The first chapter, titled "It's about business, not vanity—your book has a job to do" sets the stage for identifying what you really want to gain from authoring a book. She then follows that up with exactly what to do to make that happen. She provides templates, practical techniques, and examples for how to create a book that works for your business. Debbie talks about writing a book for one person and she made me feel like that one person. Well done!

Dan Kowalski, Solution Instigator at
Plan A Thinking, Planathinking.com

Debs is the master that can guide you to writing a book people will read. Her measured approach and experience with publishing successful books grants her the expertise that you need to tap into if you think you have a book inside you.

Tim Kist, FCMC, author and certified management consultant,
www.tk3consulting.ca

If you're going to buy just one book on how to write YOUR book – this is the one! What I LOVED about this book is its pragmatic, no-nonsense approach. Debbie Jenkins pulls no punches, she knows (don't we all) that many books start off being written as a business promotional tool – but that they don't hit the mark, and end up being nothing more than, cough, Vanity Projects! Expensive and time-consuming vanity projects. They don't offer value to the reader and they certainly don't pay back the time investment to the writer! So I was delighted to see how you can follow this straightforward format to create a book that is of value to both the readers and the writer. I also loved how visual this book is – lots of graphs and diagrams, flow charts and quirky illustrations. That makes it super-usable and very fast to get to grips with. In my past career as a PR person (I'm now a therapist and trainer), I was always telling my friends and clients to "write a book", but from now on I'll preface that advice with "read a book first" – and more specifically read THIS book.

Sue Haswell, Trainer, Coach, Psychotherapist, Author,
www.suehaswell.co.uk

Get your book out of your head and turned into a valuable asset for your business. Think of your book as a vehicle. It needs to move the reader from point A to point B and gets them over a 'hump'. And guess what, many people are struggling to get over the self-same hump! Patterns form with prospective clients, and I'm sure you've heard the same problem couched in different ways, time and time again. Your 'Asset Path' book will help you cultivate and enhance relationships and turn readers into raving (paying) fans. You just need to get over your own person hump of 'How' do I write such a book? This is where Debbie steps in! Whatever you need your book to do – save time/money, generate revenue, or increase the value of your business – you can do it with this helpful, no-nonsense book. Learn from the master!

Christine Ware, 'The Career Doctor' www.thecareerdoctor.co.uk

Stop Writing Books Nobody Reads is more than a guide to writing, it's a whole new way for leaders to think about their business and create value for their clients. Writing a book hadn't crossed my mind before meeting Debs and I didn't have a clue where to start, but this book sets out everything you need to consider in easy to follow steps. The Thought Leadership Canvas (TLC) in Chapter 2 really helped me focus in on what the reader wants to know, the A to B transformations they're looking for, how I can help solve their problems and next steps. It also helped me clarify who I was writing for and why. As Debs says, 'Forget avatars, personas, demographics. Write for one special person with the one problem that your book can solve'. I use the TLC canvas daily now to make notes during client calls, explore new ideas, write marketing content and outline proposals. Whether you're looking to crystallise your ideas or ready to break the brain-world barrier and share them, this book will give you the tools and guidance you need, challenge your thinking and make you laugh along the way.

Davina Ripton, Business Change Coach, www.changeready.co.uk

Business author? Get into a bigger game... Thousands of business books come out each year and the number is increasing, encouraged by people who coach consultants, and made easier by the digital publishing options now available. Some of these books are truly valuable – they can change the fortunes of their readers. On the other hand, many feel as if they were written to tick a box. In general, those approaching the task of writing a business book seriously under-estimate the level at which the top authors play the game. I'm not just talking about getting the words down. I mean planning, sequencing, designing the reader's journey, testing, marketing... If you want to write a really useful book, and maximise its chances of getting read and referred to, Debs' short, friendly yet authoritative book is your inside track to professional-level performance. Its most important idea: a relentless insistence on adding value for the reader.

Andy Bass, PhD, author of Start With What Works and Committed Action, bassclusker.com

The how to write a non-fiction business book guide for all wannabe business book authors.

Karen Currier, Author of *DOING intentionally*, www.currier.co.uk

Having written a few books without Deb's wise perspective, I'm looking forward to the next one being more focused and useful to the people I want to help. I recognised quite a few of the mistakes I've made, and now I know the antidote. All delivered in Deb's no-nonsense style with the benefit of her experience and humour!

Donna Higton, Life Coach and multi-author,

www.donnaonthebeach.com

What a stimulating book! I loved the message "your book needs to be so interesting that they devour it, and then they want the next one", because it helps to set the scene of creating a successful conveyor of information that people want. The clear messages about understanding the receiver of your information, to package the information so that it can be assimilated by the reader quickly (not always a book) and create the change (by writing in a way that captures the heart of the reader), are the elixirs the writer must find to achieve their goal.

Dr Eva Bhattacharyya, advocate for women in STEM,

www.prashnalife.com

This book is a wake-up call. It clearly shows you how to navigate through the writing jungle and get out of it with a huge treasure. I find Debbie's TLC model really helpful and I love the Tube Test! Such a simple test but as with many simple brilliant ideas – they can bring you the biggest breakthroughs and help you tremendously. Get this book so that you too can avoid the so many pitfalls that authors too often fall into.

Dr. Maya Novak, mindful healing expert and author of *Heal Beyond Expectations*

Whenever Debbie does anything to be honest I take an immediate intake of breath. Why? Because I know she's shaking things up and I need to ground my nervous system into getting connected with her revolutionary ideas! Time and time again she does this – turns my business world upside down in the most amazing way possible by the way and this book speaks to this again OMG does it! She has written a book which reflects the times we live in where for me at least I have too many screens, too much to read, too much information to process and too many things to do! I love how she cuts through the noise offering a zeitgeisty practical laser focussed tool in this book for me to actually give my clients a book not only that they can actually read in this lifetime (lol!) but that they want to read! This is so worthy of your attention if you are looking to get noticed in your industry and by your dream clients. Frankly, you would be 'blonde,' not to pay attention to this industry-disrupting book! It will become a seminal and movement-creating book in time, that I know for sure!

Carrie Eddins, PR & Media expert, Connection Marketing Specialist
www.theblondepreneur.com